FREEDOM
A Beautiful Choice!

BIBLICAL KEYS TO EXPERIENCING TRUE FREEDOM

Nancy Tanton

Nancy Tanton Ministries

FREEDOM – A BEAUTIFUL CHOICE
Biblical Keys To Experiencing True Freedom

Cover design by Ken Raney.

nancytantonministries@gmail.com
www.nancytantonministries.com

CONTENTS

FOREWARD

I will always remember the day I stood in the empty garage of our farmhouse, void of any hope for freedom. The person I had become was so far from the one I knew God had created me to be. Chained with past regrets, generational bondage, and bitterness, there was seemingly no way out. Yet, in my despair, I cried out to the God I had just met…the One Who promised freedom…the One Who was my only hope. To my amazement, He answered me in unimaginable ways. Over the next seven years we embarked on the journey of a lifetime. He took me on a path where each step of the way offered more and more freedom. It wasn't an easy, carefree journey; many times there were challenging, seemingly impossible choices. Yet, in His faithfulness, He provided the grace for each step of the way.

God graciously taught me truths from His Word that not only set me free, but also provided tools powerful enough to set any captive free, no matter how seemingly hopeless. He speaks in 1 John 3:8 that Jesus came to undo the works of the devil and then goes on throughout His Word to proclaim that He makes all things new – removing things from our lives that keep us bound, replacing them with new life and hope.

Within the accompanying videos and the pages of this workbook, are the lessons I learned. They are simple lessons, taken straight from God's Word. I refer to them as our "True North". John 8:32 says that as we continue in His Word, we will know the truth, and that truth will set us free. My heart's desire is that all discover the freedom Jesus died to give.

I am praying that, as you embark on your own journey, you too, will discover that freedom. May the Lord bless you and set you apart for Himself.

Nancy A. Tanton

The Bible Gateway app is an excellent tool as you transition between various translations used in this study.

LEADER'S GUIDE

The workbook *FREEDOM – A BEAUTIFUL CHOICE!* is designed for both individual and group study. It reinforces the truths taught in the accompanying video series in a tangible, everyday type setting, which aids in personal application. James 1:21 says it is the <u>implanted word</u> that is able to save your soul. The more we embed God's word in our lives, the more freedom we will experience. The individual success of the study will be determined by what you do with what you learn; therefore the workbook is an invaluable tool to aid in that process.

Most weeks will include five daily lessons; however some weeks purposefully have fewer, in order to give an opportunity to "catch up" on the previous weeks' lessons.

Below is a simple study format suggestion. Modify to fit the structure, size and personality of your group. Minimum time should be a 1 ½ hr group study.

- Prepare with Prayer – As a leader, consider it a privilege to bathe the study in prayer. You have an opportunity to reach the hearts and minds of the men and women with God's truth, giving them the ability to experience newfound freedom.

- 5-10 minutes – Meet and greet – This is a necessary tool in bonding and becoming comfortable enough to share.

- 10-15 minutes – Review last week's daily lessons. Encourage people to share the truths they learned or ask questions. At the same time, discourage any one person from dominating the discussion. (In the first session, use this time to allow each person to introduce themselves, depending upon the size of the group.)

- Watch video lesson. (approximately 45-55 minutes)

- 10 minutes - Discus video

- Prayer concerns

- Encourage participants to complete their daily lessons, and to come back ready to share.

God's Word is ABSOLUTE TRUTH!

If we want true freedom, we are going to have to do it God's way.

Matt. 23: 25 First clean the _____ of the cup and of the dish, so that

the _____ of it may become clean also.

When we allow God to clean up the heart, we soon find our actions responding.

Psalm 119:89 God's Word is _____ in heaven.

Psalm 119:105 Thy word is a lamp unto my _____ and a light unto my

_____.

Psalm 119:160 The _____ of Thy word is truth.

Psalm 33:11 The counsel of the Lord stands forever, His thoughts from

_____ to _____.

Proverbs. 30:5-6 _____ word of God is tested. …Do not _____ to

His words.

II Timothy 3:16-17 All scripture is inspired by God and is profitable for

_____, for _____, for _____, for

training in _____.

When God speaks through His word, we simply believe it and act upon it.

Acts 16: 23-26 Paul and Silas were in an inner prison, praying and singing

hymns of praise to God, and the prisoners were listening to them. Suddenly

there came a great earthquake, so that the _____ of

the prison house were shaken; and immediately all the doors were opened, and

_____ chains were unfastened."

WEEK ONE - FREEDOM TO LIVE THE CHRISTIAN LIFE

In the same manner that God shook the foundation of the prison, Jesus shook the very foundation of Satan's house...setting prisoners free.

I John 3:8 ...The Son of God appeared for this purpose, to _____ the works of the devil.

Romans 4:17 ...Abraham believed God, who calls into being that which does _____ _____.

I Corinthians 1:28 God chose the things that are not, that He might _____ the things that are.

Hebrews 2:14 ...Through His death, Jesus rendered the devil _____.

John 10:10 The thief comes to _____, _____, and _____; I came that they might have _____, and have it _____.

Matthew 16:18 ...upon this rock I will build my _____ and the gates of _____ shall _____ _____ against it.

Colossians. 1:12 giving thanks to the _____ Who has _____ us to share in the _____ of the saints in light.

Colossians 1: 13-14 For He delivered us from the domain of _____ and _____ us to the kingdom of His beloved Son, in whom we have _____, the _____ of sins.

Where has the enemy blinded our minds? What truths are we missing? Let's find out!!!

NOTES:

Week One - Freedom To Live the Christian Life

Stories have the ability to take abstract issues and bring them into real life circumstances. I love stories – sometimes. Now that our children are grown and away from home, they possess the freedom to let me in on some of their little childhood secrets. Take for instance the time two of my daughters roller skated in our upstairs hallway that lacked banisters and railings for the stairwell. As if skating wasn't dangerous enough, they proceeded to tell me they would "jump" the stairwell from one side to the other with "no problem". I began to realize the importance of my prayers for God to station angels around that stairwell. I also had to quietly smile at my assumption that the angels were probably bored standing there all day and night. If the truth were told, they probably requested to be stationed there because of the entertainment provided them, as well as the frequent opportunities to use their angelic gifts of rescue.

There was another story that I just recently heard that kept me awake that night thinking of all of the "what ifs". Our son and his family were here for the holidays. The children and grandpa had gone to bed and I was sitting quietly, relishing one of the late night conversations with Patrick and his precious wife, Lanitha. "Mom, I don't know if I ever told you about the time…" and he hadn't. He was joining a group of guys for a late night game of street basketball. There was a light near the basketball goal that needed to be turned on. They opened the breaker box and Patrick proceeded to feel around for the light switch; however, instead he touched a live wire. His hand immediately froze to the wire, and he could feel the electricity surging into his hand and up his arm. He said he knew that when it hit his heart it would kill him, but there was nothing he could do about it. He couldn't get his hand released from the very thing that would kill him. To this day, he doesn't know which one of the guys did it, but someone must have realized what was going on and ran to him and, in shoving him, released him from the live wire. It saved his life.

That night I kept thinking of all the different scenarios that could have played out. The fact that Patrick was sitting quietly in the chair telling me his story was proof that he had been rescued. In the same way that there had to be angelic activity to keep my silly daughters safe, I knew that somehow God had sent an angel to rescue my son. He worked through the arms and feet of another young man, but I knew it was an act of God that rescued him.

There are times in our lives that we find ourselves unable to detach ourselves from the very power that is destroying us.

Patrick's story reminds me of each one of us. There are times in our lives that we find ourselves unable to detach ourselves from the very power that is destroying us. There is nothing we can do to save ourselves. That's where the reality of God's great love is made manifest. Ephesians 2: 4-5 speaks to this. Look it up and write it here.

WEEK ONE - FREEDOM TO LIVE THE CHRISTIAN LIFE

While we were yet sinners, God sent His Son to rescue us from the power of the enemy. Sometimes, as Christians, we realize we have been rescued from the power of hell, but we fall short of recognizing the full extent of the rescue. Patrick was rescued one night, but that rescue wasn't about just one night. It provided an opportunity to live for many years to come. That was a physical rescue. The rescue that Jesus provides is so much more…and even more than just a rescue that comes into play once we die. Again turning to the scriptures, let's see what Colossians 1: 13-14 says about this.

This study is designed to reveal truths that will empower us to walk in new found freedom.

What does that Kingdom of Light look like? What difference does it make in our life? What is the real story that is trying to be told? Galatians 5:1 speaks of the very heart of God. Record it here.

We will use the scriptures as our "true north". Our current mind-sets will be constantly challenged.

It is God's intense love for us that desires to see His children walking in the freedom He purchased for them. He begs us to not only walk in it, but to refuse anything that hinders us from that continuous walk. As we just read, He rescued us from the kingdom of darkness and transferred us into the Kingdom of his dear Son, who purchased our freedom and forgave our sins. (Colossians 1: 13-14 NLT)

This study is designed to reveal truths that will empower us to walk in new found freedom. Romans 5: 17 says God has given His children the opportunity to reign in life through Jesus. We are going to look closely to what that means…how do we reign in life…what does that look like?…what does that require of me personally?

We will use the scriptures as our "true north". Our current mind-sets will be constantly challenged. God's word is so amazing! There is no other foundation that can be laid. Jesus tells us in Luke 6:46-49 that the storms of life will come to all of us. Whether we are able to remain standing will depend upon what we have built our house upon. His main message in those verses is that hearing is not enough. The real issue at hand is what we do with what He says. Turn to James 1:22-25 in your bible. Summarize what that is telling you personally.

This study is designed to give each person the opportunity to see what God's word says about a full range of life topics; however, the individual success of the study will be determined by what you do with what you learn. God has promised freedom and made it available to each one of us. He is so loving; yet, He is a gentleman. Deuteronomy 30: 19-20 says He sets before us life and death, the blessing and the curse, then allows us to make the choice. Luke 6: 46-49 tells us the consequences of that choice. So let's begin by looking up that scripture and summarizing it here.

The individual success of the study will be determined by what you do with what you learn.

The same storms will hit no matter what foundation we decide to use. The difference is that one foundation leads to destruction and the other leads to life.

In our time together this week, we saw what God says about His Word. It is settled in heaven, which means it is eternally true (Psalm 119:89). What truths, then, do we need to know that will bring the victories of heaven into our daily life? What are those mysteries God desires to reveal to us?

Let's begin with Colossians 1:26-27. Look it up and write it below.

Colossians 1: 27 tells us God's mystery is that our hope is Christ in us.
What does that mean to you?

WEEK ONE - FREEDOM TO LIVE THE CHRISTIAN LIFE

This word has been a foundational scripture in my life. Romans 7:18 tells me that there is no good thing dwelling in my flesh – if I look to myself, I have no hope. But Acts 17:28 says that in Him I live and move and have my being. That is where my hope lies. Galatians 2:20 says that when I accepted Christ as my Savior I died to my old self and accepted the Life of Christ to live and reign in my body. That is God's mystery that has been revealed. That is where my hope lies. Christ in me. Greater is He that is in you than he that is in the world (I John 4:4). I cannot change myself. Only God can change me. However, the one thing I can do…the one thing that is absolutely essential…is that I have the power of choice. God honors our choice. If I choose Life…if I choose to obey His word…then the storms of life will only be used to mold me deeper and deeper into the image of His Son. If I choose my own way then God will honor that choice and allow me to have my own way…but that way is a dead end street full of futility and destruction.

Take a look at Deuteronomy 30:19. Write it below.

When I accepted Christ as my Savior I died to my old self and accepted the Life of Christ to live and reign in my body.

If I choose to obey His word…then the storms of life will only be used to mold me deeper and deeper into the image of His Son.

How does verse 20 say we choose life?

Take time to journal your thoughts and decisions. Then use those thoughts to guide you in prayer.

Living in the country definitely had its advantages. There were always wide open spaces for imaginations to run freely. No store bought items were needed when company came. The children immediately scattered to their favorite spots to begin their self designated assignment – stick house building. The wooded area provided just the right place to build them! Sticks were gathered, brush was cleared away, rooms were created, and more added as the plans grew. All day long the project was at the forefront of every child's mind. Nothing else mattered. These were not your ordinary stick houses, mind you. They were masterpieces. Only problem - they became so involved in building the house that they never finished to enjoy the fruit of their labors.

Sometimes our lives can become like those houses. We try so hard to frame a life that can hold everything we think will produce happiness and contentment. The trouble is, when we successfully finish one room, our focus starts wandering to another and another because the very thing we were confident would bring success in the beginning didn't produce the fulfillment we expected.

Adam and Eve were in the garden and everything was perfect. They had everything they could possibly need, including amazing intimacy with God. They were actually able to meet with Him and speak with Him face to face. Even then, though, they still had the ability to choose. When the enemy took Eve's eyes off of what she had, and placed them on "more sticks" that could make her world so much bigger, she fell for the lie. She bought into the deception that God didn't love her enough to have her best interest at heart. She doubted the God Who created her and gave her to Adam – the One who placed them at the very center of His world.

The God Who created choice now honored that choice. If evil had not been allowed there would have been no choice, but **the absence of choice only creates a puppet, not a relationship**. The same is true in our lives as well. God delivered us from the kingdom of darkness into the Kingdom of His Son, but He never took away our right to choose.

The absence of choice only creates a puppet, not a relationship.

If our choice is to be a vessel of honor, we need to build our house (or vessel) rightly.

Find II Timothy 2: 20-21 in your bible. As you write verse 21 below, consider the seriousness of the choice God is putting before us. If our choice is to be a vessel of honor, we need to build our house (or vessel) rightly. Paul said in I Corinthians 3:10 that he was very careful to lay a proper foundation. Tomorrow we will study that foundation, but before the foundation is laid, the design must come first. God told Jeremiah that before He formed him in the womb, He knew him and set him apart for a certain purpose (Jeremiah 1:5). In the same way, God is very specific in His intentions for us. Look up the scripture references below and write them out; then journal what God is saying to you personally. Hopefully we will capture a theme as we realize God's loving design for our personal lives.

II Timothy 2: 21

Romans 12:2

How do we become transformed?

What we subject
our mind to will
greatly influence our
thinking..

Our mind is a vital part of God's design. Whether we receive stimuli through seeing, hearing, touching, smelling or tasting, those sensory perceptions are filtered through our mind. It has a memory where it stores all previous experiences and knowledge. However, our mind doesn't have a mind of its own (excuse the pun). We have trained our mind what to think, what to accept, and what to reject. That's what life does. It trains us. **What we subject our mind to will greatly influence our thinking.** If we live our life as the world lives, our minds will conform to the ways of the world. In the end, we become what God calls a vessel of dishonor. God's design for a vessel of honor requires a transformed mind...one that runs everything through scripture to see if it's true and acceptable. Look up Philippians 4:8. List the guidelines for our thinking - Whatever is...

What correlation do you see between this verse and Romans 12:2?

John 8: 31-32 (NASB) "...If you _____ in My word, then you are

_____ of Mine and you will know the _____ and the

_____ will set you free.

How do we become disciples?

What is required for us to know the truth so deeply that it sets us free?

We will look at two scriptures together beginning with Galatians 5:1. Record it below.

Look up II Corinthians 3:17. How do the two scriptures relate to each other?
(Looking at Zechariah 4:6 might give a clue.)

Philippians 4: 6-7 is a lengthy scripture but worth writing out. Think about each part as you write it.

What, if any, anxious thoughts keeps troubling you? Take time to tell God about them. Don't forget to thank Him for hearing you, loving you and moving on your behalf.

Look up and write Romans 8:2

As we spend time in His word we begin to think His thoughts, dream His dreams and find His freedom.

The law of gravity is a natural law that governs our entire world. You will experience that law whether you live in Kansas or California, Kenya or America. We can depend on that fact. However, every day we see airplanes flying in the sky, defying that law. There is actually a law that supersedes the law of gravity – the law of aerodynamics. Notice I said "supersedes", not "cancels". The law of gravity is still there. If the pilot turns off his engines the law of gravity is once again in force.

The bible says there is a law of sin and death. Romans 6:16,23 states that the soul that sins will die. That's true if you live in America or the remotest part of the earth. Nothing can change that – it's the law. HOWEVER!!!! There is a higher law. Romans 3:27 says we are made righteous through the law of faith. Our above scripture says that law of faith in Christ Jesus sets us free from the law of sin and death. Just as the airplane is free to fly when it comes under the proper law, we too are free to fly out from under the law that seeks to kill us. It's a free gift. We don't undo or cancel the old law; we simply change kingdoms where that law ceases to exist.

These scriptures show God's amazing love. He desires that we walk in complete freedom. He alone knows how to accomplish that. As we spend time in His word we begin to think His thoughts, dream His dreams and find His freedom. The world makes many empty boasts and promises, but in the end they fail. Only God offers true freedom for every area of our lives…freedom from deep within that is independent of people or circumstances. What a beautiful design!!

Take time today to talk to God about His design for you. Go ahead. Don't be afraid to ask Him what it looks like…and after you ask….listen. He just might tell you something you have longed to hear.

My husband and I drove through a neighborhood development last week and noticed lots of future homes. We didn't actually see the homes – we saw basements poured and foundations laid. That was a sure sign to us that the houses were soon to be built. God doesn't talk too much about basements, but He has a lot to say about foundations. I Corinthians 3:11 says "No man can lay a foundation other than the one which is laid, which is Jesus Christ." We also read in Luke 6: 46-49 that the end result of our lives depends upon the foundation we lay. It is evident from those verses that we will all experience some pretty strong storms in our lives. Our foundation will determine what those storms are allowed to accomplish. If we lay that foundation on the things the world offers (sand), the storms will bring devastation and ruin. If we lay our foundation on the rock (Jesus), when the storms of life hit, everything that has been built upon that rock will still be standing at the end of the day.

The question then is "What does Jesus as our foundation look like?" What is it about Him that will allow us to stand when the storm looks like it will take us under? When Jesus was in the midst of a storm with his disciples, He simply spoke to the storm and the winds obeyed. Can we do the same? If so, what do we speak when those storms hit? What truths can give us firm footing? Using the scriptures as our "True North", let's begin to answer those questions.

The first question we need to ask is "Why do the storms come?" Romans 5: 3-5, James 1: 2-4 and I Peter 1: 6-7 tell us to rejoice when we encounter trials because there is a reason for them. It would be good to stop and read those references. God wants to purify our character and strengthen our faith. His ultimate goal with each one of us is that we be conformed into the image of His Son. It would be great if we could be conformed into that image through an easy life. I want to protect my children from hardships, yet I want to see them grow in their faith. When I'm honest I know that I grew the most during those difficult times when I was crying out to God and saw Him as my only Hope. That's why it says that the way to true hope can only be found through the tribulation route. God's purpose for our storms, however, is in direct contrast to our enemy who seeks to use those same storms to destroy us. He desires to create trauma and fear so we doubt God's goodness, faithfulness and power. When the storms hit, God's word tells us to speak to our souls and say, "Peace. Be Still." God is doing a good work and I need to cooperate with Him so His will can be accomplished. The enemy wants us to speak despair and defeat. Let's begin planting our feet on life-giving truth.

His ultimate goal with each one of us is that we be conformed into the image of His Son.

I grew the most during those difficult times when I was crying out to God and saw Him as my only Hope.

Jesus came to destroy the works of the devil.

I John 3:8 (NASB) "When people keep on sinning, it shows that they belong to the devil, who has been sinning since the beginning. But the Son of God appeared for

this purpose, that He might _____ the _____

This study will look at many ways Satan tries to destroy our lives. We will discover his schemes, but also realize that Jesus came to destroy those works. No matter what the enemy has done in our lives, God has a way out. This part of our foundation is the truth that JESUS CAME TO DESTROY THE WORKS OF THE DEVIL.

When we recognize areas in our lives where the enemy has set up camp, we can bring those areas to Jesus and appropriate His word that proclaims He has destroyed the enemy's hold. We will also learn of ways we open the door to the enemy, so that we can close those doors once and for all. This verse promises hope for freedom – and freedom tastes so good!

Write John 10:10

Satan will steal, kill or destroy any area in your life that he can. Jesus came to destroy those evil works so we can live an abundant life. What are some areas in your life where you see the enemy working?

Ask Jesus to come into those areas and guide you into the freedom He purchased.

Read Romans 4:16-17. God made Abraham a father of many nations. When we accept Christ as our Lord and Savior, you and I become a part of that. We are descendants of Abraham; therefore, all of his promises belong to us. Fill in the blanks for the last part of verse 17 below. I like how the NASB version says it. He (Abraham) believed,

even _____ who gives _____ to the _____ and calls

into being that which _____.

I love the part that says, "God gives life to the dead and calls into being that which does not exist." No matter what our former life lacked - whether we lacked a parent's love, the ability to learn, acceptance of peers – whatever, God can call that into being as though it was always there. He does it through His Word as we discover who we really are and the depth of His love. Everyone has a story. Is there a place in your life where you need God to touch and restore? If so, take time to talk to Him about it right now. You may find it easier to journal. Whichever way, He is waiting and anxious to show you His love and power.

I Corinthians 1:27-28 is the counterpart to the verse in Romans. Write verse 28 below.

Not only can God bring into being those things that never existed, but He can take the "things that are" and make them as though they never were. Notice He doesn't say He takes them away and they never did exist. That would be pretending that reality never existed. Instead, He can take away the pain, the torture, the works the enemy did through circumstances and people. God can bring complete healing and restoration into our lives in spite of the circumstances. This study is designed to be interactive with others, but more importantly to be interactive with God. Take time to talk to Him about your life, your dreams, successes, failures, hurts…and let Him begin to make all things new.

God can bring complete healing and restoration into our lives in spite of the circumstances.

Hebrews 2:14 (NASB) Therefore, since the children share in flesh and blood, He

(Jesus) Himself likewise also partook of the same that through _____

He might render _____ him who had the power of death, that is, the

_____.

Jesus came to destroy the things the devil has already done in our lives; however, this verse goes a step further. We no longer need to be subjected to his constant bombardment. God longs for us to accept the truth that Jesus rendered the devil powerless in our lives. Once we accept Jesus as our Lord and Savior, this is our inheritance. No longer are we slaves of a wicked ruler but instead are children of the King with all that legacy includes.

Two scriptures in Matthew will serve for our one last point today. Look at Matthew 16: 18-19 and Matthew 18:18. Write Matthew 18:18 below.

I love the way different versions use different words in two places here. King James and other translations use the words bind and loose. The side notes of the New American Standard Version (NASB) and the Living Bible both use forbid and permit. It helps me realize the meaning of some rather ancient language. If we take these scriptures literally, they will empower us, but also cause great caution with our words. It is another scripture we will delve into during our studies. It holds precious nuggets we won't want to miss

THROUGH THESE SCRIPTURES WE REALIZE THAT JESUS

    1) CAME TO DESTROY THE DEVIL'S WORKS,
    2) CAN CALL INTO BEING THINGS THAT NEVER EXISTED;
    3) MAKES THINGS THAT EXIST AS THOUGH THEY NEVER EXISTED;
    4) RENDERS THE DEVIL POWERLESS IN OUR LIVES;
    5) HAS GIVEN US THE AUTHORITY TO ENACT THOSE PROMISES.

"O the depth of the riches both of the wisdom and knowledge of God! How unsearchable are His judgments and His ways past finding out! (Romans 11:33)" We serve a mighty God; nothing is impossible for Him. As we continue abiding (living) in His Word He will continue revealing Himself to us. We've only just begun!...

Jesus said it does no good to clean up the outside if the inside is full of sin. God isn't interested in watching us put on our righteous face in public if our heart is unchanged. Therefore we must ask ourselves, how does the inside get clean? We will see that accomplishing a clean heart requires action from two sides – God's side and ours. Let's take a closer look.

In I Corinthians, Paul warns us to be careful how we build upon our foundation. There is only one foundation that will assure us of eternal life, which is Jesus Christ. Once we have laid that foundation; however, there are a variety of materials we can use to start building. It reminds me of the story of the three little pigs. The question each of them faced was how much time and energy were they willing to put into building their house. We see the first pig hurriedly and carelessly erecting a straw house. He didn't have to go far to get the straw, and tying it into place must have been fairly easy. The problem was that when the enemy came knocking at his door, he had nothing to defend himself. He was an easy target. One puff was all it took. The second pig was a bit more energetic and possibly a tiny bit more deliberate. He went out to find some sticks, and designed a house that could easily be erected but a bit more stable. However, he too was an easy target for the enemy. Perhaps the wolf had to blow a bit harder, but that was no problem for him. Two or three puffs and down it went.

Now we come to the third pig. He knew about the enemy and also knew what he needed to do to protect himself from an eminent attack. Making bricks was not an easy task. It took time and labor, yet he was willing to do whatever was necessary to successfully foil that enemy who would surely come knocking on his door. We know the rest of the story. Fortunately for the other two, the third pig graciously allowed them to enter into his home for the protection they needed. If he had been as foolish as the other two, none of them would have survived the attacks.

I Corinthians 3:13 tells us God will reveal each of our works. The purpose of the fire He sends into our lives is to reveal the truth about our building materials. If it is the wood, hay and stubble, we will discover we have no usable weapon against the enemy of our souls. As the Lord reveals our true condition, we have a choice – walk in rebellion or accept the opportunity to repent and surrender. With repentance comes the gift of forgiveness and possible restoration.

Life lessons reveal our true state. Even when we are certain our building materials are gold, silver or precious stones, there is usually a mixture in the product. In this case, God uses the fire to separate the precious from the dross. With the wood, hay and stubble, the solution can only be to burn up the entire structure. However, if we have used the better materials, the fire comes not to destroy, but to separate the dross (impurities) so we can partner with God to remove them. Exposing the dross is God's business; deciding to separate and rid ourselves of it lies within our own hands. Remember, God constantly gives us a choice, then honors that choice.

The purpose of the fire He sends into our lives is to reveal the truth about our building materials.

As the Lord reveals our true condition, we have a choice – walk in rebellion or accept the opportunity to repent and surrender.

Exposing the dross is God's business; deciding to separate and rid ourselves of it lies within our own hands.

The Design…The Foundation… The Building… that's the way God rolls.

I Corinthians 3:10-15 will be our guideline for building on the foundation. Read it through three times and then summarize it below.

Matthew 23: 25-26 shows us where the real test will be evaluated.
What is Jesus saying here?

What does Proverbs 25:4 tell us if we will separate the dross from the silver?

Mark 4:14-20 speaks about the different soils, but it carries the same message. It's worth the read. There were those who were not even interested in the condition of their soil. When the seed came, Satan easily took it away (one puff) and it was gone. (verse 15)

Those who received it but did not care for it properly, were soon met with the trials of life. The enemy convinced them the word they received was not true, and they fell away. The cares of the world and the deceitfulness of riches choked the word out of other hearts. (Two puffs and they're down for the count.) (verses 17-19)

Those who received, cultivated and cared for the Word produced much fruit. They were able to endure the storms that came trying to destroy the live-giving seed. (verse 20) That brings us full circle to the trials we will unavoidably face in life. As we get this truth imbedded deep within our soul, we will respond more readily to the scriptures that instruct us to consider it all joy when those trials come…knowing God's purpose is to mold us more and more closely into the image of His Son.

WHAT WE NEED TO KNOW BEFORE WE BEGIN BUILDING:

What reason does Isaiah 5:13 give for God's people going into captivity and perishing?

Lack of knowledge puts us in the category of the first soil. We have no foundation and are easily taken captive. The Holy Spirit desires to guide us into all the truth by taking us to God's Word. (John 14:26) Let's allow that Word to speak to us once more.

Who is our adversary in I Peter 5:8 and what do we need to know about him?

The first two pigs didn't take their enemy into account. They simply wanted to quickly build a house so they could relax and enjoy life. It takes time and focus to rightly build. **What might be keeping you from focusing on your most important house?**

Ephesians 4: 17-18 speaks to the standard we set as truth. What is the result if we choose to walk as the world walks and think as the world thinks?

WEEK ONE - FREEDOM TO LIVE THE CHRISTIAN LIFE

Hardness of heart begins by walking in the futile mindset of the world. It then causes us to ignorantly become excluded from the life of God. Peter warns about the presence of a real enemy seeking to destroy whomever he can.

An excellent scripture to address this is Psalms 139: 23-24 (NASB)

_____- me, O God, and know my _____;

_____ me and know my _____ _____; And

see if there be any _____ way in me, and _____ me in the

_____ way.

Consider the reason you might have for struggling to give proper attention to God and His Word. God doesn't want empty promises. He doesn't even want you to try to clean yourself. What He desires is a surrendered heart to the Only One possessing the power to reach the very inner depths where the change must be made. Take this opportunity to ask Him to begin or continue the process of cleaning the inside of the cup.

Water from a clean cup tastes so good!

WEEK ONE - FREEDOM TO LIVE THE CHRISTIAN LIFE

I like stories. There are times I would rather sit and listen to stories than face everyday life. I'm not a novel reader. I love books that teach me about the love and power of God. However, even in those I can get lost in the book without using it as a tool in my life. What about you? Are there days you would rather snuggle down and just let the world go by? My oldest daughter Stephanie had an opportunity to accompany her husband Dean on a business trip to California a few years ago. The company provided a beautiful suite with luxurious accommodations. As Dean attended the business meetings, Stephanie was able to remain behind and enjoy all the amenities. When she decided to try the pool, the doting attendant asked her "sun or shade?", "would you like something to drink?" "is there anything I can do to make your stay more enjoyable"? Who wouldn't like an opportunity like that?!!! The first few days were relaxing and great fun…a lifestyle so easy to slip into…a lifestyle of "ME". As she began to look around at others also pampering themselves, she saw the danger of the temptation. If she, as well as they, would embrace that lifestyle, not as a few days of fun and relaxation but an everyday habit, their lives would become one of total futility. It really wouldn't matter if they lived or died. They would not make any impact on the world because they would only be consumed with themselves. Life wasn't meant to be lived for ourselves. There is no fulfillment or reward in doing that. Neither is life meant to be spent in a book. It is meant to be lived… and if we are going to live life, we soon discover there is an enemy fighting against us. What does that enemy look like? What are his credentials? We're going to look very closely at that…but first of all, here's a story…..

Sam finally got into the game. He had waited all season for the coach to give him the signal but it never came. Today was the day and now was the time. He excitedly scrambled to the officials' table to check in and waited for the whistle to blow. In a series of unforeseen proportions, three players had fouled out, two had been hurt and the coach was forced to put in the last player on the bench. It certainly wasn't what he wanted. The score was tied in the fourth quarter. He really needed his star players on the court. Sam saw this as an opportunity to show his stuff! His team had possession of the ball so now was his chance. The forward dribbled down the court passing to the point guard who passed to another player and then another, who shot the ball…no basket and the opposing team got the rebound. Only seconds remained as Sam guarded his man. Now it was their forward who took the ball down the court, passing back and forth until there was opportunity for a shot. Tensions ran high…and then…Sam's man had the ball and was preparing to shoot. Sam tried blocking the shot, but instead fouled his opponent. The ball missed the hoop but the other team now had an opportunity to win through free throws, which they did. Instead of being the hero, Sam was now the enemy. Failing to recognize other previously missed shots or fouls committed that brought the team to this point, they only saw the last few seconds of the game. For them, it was entirely his fault.

Life is like that sometimes. We get dealt a hard hand and look around to see why. Too often our sight is limited to one area, when that really isn't the real issue at all. Our problem is not the circumstance, but our limited eyesight. It can sometimes even be our position from where we are looking. We all have an enemy, but the scriptures tell us the enemy isn't people or circumstances. The enemy has managed to hide behind those in order to remain safe and in control. Today we are going to look at the real enemy…our real opponent. In order to do that, we are going to have to recognize not only our enemy, but also our correct position of battle.

Life wasn't meant to be lived for ourselves.

Too often our sight is limited to one area, when that really isn't the real issue at all.

WEEK ONE - FREEDOM TO LIVE THE CHRISTIAN LIFE

The purpose of this study is four-fold. We need to 1.) recognize where the battle is located 2.) identify the enemy. 3) know where our position and responsibility lie; and 4). appropriate the authority Jesus has over all things.

We will use several scriptures that are written below as our rulebook. This is a rather heavy, but necessary lesson. Without it, we might as well snuggle up and read a book. Stick with me. It's that foundation stuff…put on your work boots and let's get started.

Our enemy is not people or circumstances

This is an extremely important lesson. **I HAVE PROVIDED A WORKSHEET ON THE LAST PAGE OF THIS LESSON THAT INCLUDES ALL THE REFERENCED SCRIPTURES BELOW.** We will correlate these verses to obtain a clear view of the battle, our enemy and our ultimate victory. We will underline, circle, box in, and draw a zigzag cloud around certain scriptures to aid in correlating them. You might prefer highlighting. Let's begin:

Where does Ephesians 3:10 & 6:12 tell us our enemy is located?

_____ Underline "in the heavenly places" in both verses.

Where is Christ seated? (Ephesians 1:20) _____ Underline

that. Before we go any farther, please notice although the enemy and Christ are both in heavenly places, Jesus is FAR ABOVE the enemy. We don't have an enemy equal to or stronger than God. Also look at I Peter 3:22 and underline where Jesus is seated.

We see the good guys and the bad guys are "up there" duking it out. That's where the battle lies, but where are we in this mix? Look at Ephesians 2: 5-6 and underline where we are now seated. YIKES!!! …but wait – there is no need to worry. 2 Corinthians 10: 3-4 tells us we are not defenseless against the enemy. God has empowered us with divinely powerful weapons (you might call them spiritual blessings). Where does Eph 1:3 say

these spiritual blessings are located? _____ Underline it.

Let's review: Our enemy is not people or circumstances; our enemy is located in heavenly places. Jesus is also located in heavenly places, but HE IS FAR ABOVE ALL THINGS. We are seated in heavenly places with Jesus and are equipped with divinely powerful weapons to use against the enemy. So far so good!

We might call this next segment the *Circle Section*…

What do we need to know about the enemy? We already know it is not people, but what does he look like? Does he have a name? Get ready to circle…or change highlighters.

Ephesians 6:12 answers that question. Circle the words that describe our enemy.

Who does Ephesians 1:21 tell us Christ reigns over? _____

_____

I Peter 3:22 verifies that. Circle the enemies in both scriptures. Notice again where they are located.

In Colossians 1:16 we find that all things were created through Christ. Circle the words that would describe our enemy. As we do that, it helps us to realize the power structure. We see thrones, dominions, rulers and authorities as the created, not the creator. **God, through Christ, created all things.**

Col 2: 13-15 describes the enemy Jesus disarmed. Circle the names given the enemy.

Finally (for the circled section), who is the enemy in Ephesians 3:10 that needs to be addressed?

Did you notice the common names in each of the verses? Write them here_____

_____

God wants to make sure we realize who the real enemy is. The good news is that Jesus has conquered them ALL! Another happy ending...

Now for the *Box Section*

This section is absolutely essential. Who are we? The enemy knows if he can steal our identity, he can steal our inheritance. Colossians 1: 12 reveals that God is the one who qualifies us to share in our inheritance. We become His children when we acknowledge Jesus as our Lord and Savior. It is not because of our own righteousness, but because we have now entered into His righteousness (Galatians 2:20). God calls this the mystery of godliness. He does the work, we inherit the blessing. What a God!!!

"In Him we live and move and have our being." (Acts 17:28) Ephesians 4: 15 reveals the more we "grow up" INTO HIM, the more we can recognize and act upon this truth. Put a box around INTO HIM.

Because we are in Him and He is in us, we were raised WITH HIM and are seated WITH HIM. Place a box around those two places in Ephesians 2: 5-6

Because of our relationship IN CHRIST, we are blessed with every spiritual blessing. Box in that truth in Ephesians 1:3

Colossians 2: 13-15 reminds us God made us alive together _____.
That deserves another box.

The enemy knows if he can steal our identity, he can steal our inheritance.

27

Finally, Eph 3:10 tells us that we (the church) are the ones who speak to the rulers and authorities in the heavenly places. WE DON'T HAVE TO ENGAGE THE ENEMY. WE SIMPLY MAKE KNOWN TO THEM WHAT WAS ACCOMPLISHED ON OUR BEHALF.

With that realization, church, it's time for us to grow up!! We need to put our books down and step into real life. Col 1:16 and Col 2: 13-15 catch a glimpse of the whole truth (God calls it His manifold wisdom). All things are created by Him and subject to Him. When we were still living in sin, Christ died for us. He forgave all our sins, CANCEL-ING OUT ALL DECREES THAT WERE WRITTEN AGAINST US by nailing them to the cross. HE DISARMED THE RULERS AND AUTHORITIES through that act. They no longer have any power over us. What a glorious revelation! It's time to pick up our weapons and use them to enforce what God has accomplished for us.

Final Segment - THE ZIG ZAG CLOUD SECTION.

Ephesians 1:21 states Christ is _____ all rule, authority, power and dominion. Mark it with a victory cloud.

I Peter 3:22 says all angels, authorities and powers have been_____

_____. Mark those last three words.

Eph 4:15 says Christ is the _____. Deserves another victory cloud.

Col 1:16 declares all things have been created _____ and

_____. He is before _____. Col 2: 13-15 states He

has _____ the rulers and authorities, He made a _____

_____, having _____ over them.

Mark each of those verses.

A final summarization might be appropriate. This is probably our most intense study, but as we understand the ground rules, we will be able to stand where we need to stand, see what we need to see and do what we need to do. Let's speak to the four original points.

1). Where is the battle located?
The battle is totally in the heavenly realm, and must be fought with the divinely pow-erful weapons God has given.

2). Who is the enemy?

The enemy is called many names: rulers, powers, authorities, world forces, spiritual forces, dominion. These names describe what his intention is. – to dominate and rule.

3). What is our position and responsibility?

We are seated with Christ in the heavenly places where WE are to speak to the rulers and authorities, declaring to them the victory that was won at the cross.

4). How do we appropriate the authority Jesus has over all things?

God's Word is living and active and sharper than any two edged sword. It is the sword of the Spirit which is the Word of God. Therefore, we take the authority of His Word and declare it to the enemy. Jesus told us in Matthew 18:18 "Whatever YOU forbid on earth shall be forbidden in heaven and whatever YOU permit on earth shall be permitted in heaven." James 1:22-24 admonishes us to be doers of the word and not hearers only. We've "heard" a lot of the word through this lesson. **LET'S GO DO IT!! ....end of story........or perhaps just the beginning............**

Whatever YOU forbid on earth shall be forbidden in heaven and whatever YOU permit on earth shall be permitted in heaven.

EPHESIANS 6:12 Our struggle is against rulers, powers, world forces and spiritual forces in the heavenly places.

EPHESIANS 1:20-21 God seated Christ in the heavenly places FAR ABOVE all rule, authority, power and dominion.

I PETER 3:22 Jesus is at the right hand of God, having gone into heaven, after angels and authorities and powers HAD BEEN SUBJECTED TO HIM.

Ephesians 2: 5-6 God saved us by His grace and then raised us up WITH HIM, and seated us WITH HIM in the heavenly places in Christ Jesus.

2 CORINTHIANS 10:4 For the weapons of our warfare are not of the flesh, but divinely powerful for the destruction of fortresses.

EPHESIANS 1:3 God has blessed us with every spiritual blessing in the heavenly places in Christ.

EPHESIANS 4:15 We are to GROW UP in all aspects INTO HIM, Who is the head, even Christ.

COLOSSIANS 1:16 For IN HIM all things were created, both in the heavens and on earth, visible and invisible, whether thrones or dominions or rulers or authorities – all things have been created THROUGH Him and FOR HIM. HE is BEFORE ALL THINGS AND IN HIM all things hold together.

COLOSSIANS 2: 13-15 when you were dead in your transgressions and the uncircumcision of your flesh HE made you alive together WITH HIM, having forgiven us all our transgressions, having cancelled out the certificate of debt consisting of decrees against us and which was hostile to us...nailing it to the cross. When HE had disarmed the rulers and authorities, HE made a public display of them, having triumphed over them THROUGH HIM.)

EPHESIANS 3: 10 The manifold wisdom of God is made known THROUGH THE CHURCH(us) to the rulers and authorities in the heavenly places.

FREEDOM Through Forgiveness

FORGIVENESS IS <u>NOT</u> SAYING THAT WHAT SOMEONE DID WAS _____ or

_____

FORGIVENESS IS <u>NOT</u> AN _____ – IT <u>IS</u> A _____

ONCE YOU FORGIVE, GOD CAN HEAL THE HURT CAUSED BY THE ACTION.

Matthew 18:21-22 Forgiveness is not a _____ – it is an _____

Matthew 18: 26 & 29 Both servants asked, "Have _____ with me and I

will _____

Matthew 18: 27 The King had _____ and _____ the debt.

Matthew 18: 30 The ungrateful servant was _____

Matthew 18: 35 When we refuse to forgive, God hands us over to the

_____.

Colossians 3: 13 We are to forgive as _____ _____ us.

   1. We did not _____ to be forgiven.

   2. We could not _____ for what we have done.

   3. Christ forgave us _____ we asked;

   4. Forgave before we_____ forgiveness or _____

     we needed it;

   5. We are to _____ _____

31

Week Two - Freedom Through Forgiveness

Isaiah 59:1, 2 Our sins _____ us from God

Hebrews 12:15 Bitterness _____ many and can cause others to

come _____ of the _____ of God.

Matthew 18:18 Whatever you _____ on earth is _____ in

heaven; Whatever you _____ on earth is _____ in heaven.

Ephesians 4:32 Be _____ to one another, tender-hearted,

_____ one another, even as _____ in _____

forgave you.

Ephesians 4: 26-27 Anger gives the _____ an opportunity.

NO ONE CAN MAKE YOU ANGRY. THEY SIMPLY GIVE YOU AN OPPORTUNITY TO BE ANGRY. YOU ARE THE ONE WHO MAKES THE CHOICE.

Get alone with God and ask Him to bring to mind anyone you need to forgive…Little and big things alike. Phil 4:13 – You can forgive everyone through Christ! You can't depend on your feelings. God doesn't need your feelings. He only needs your willingness to forgive.

Forgiveness is not passive. You can't just let the situation slip by until you think you've forgotten it. It goes INWARD instead of leaving. You have to look at that situation and CHOOSE to forgive that person, to forgive God, or anyone else (including yourself!)

Then, once you have forgiven, ask God to bring healing into your life in that area.

Eccl 7: 20-22 Indeed, there is not a righteous person on earth who continually does good and who never sins.

NOTES:

We need to state some facts before we even begin our lesson today. It will help us go where we need to go.

1. FORGIVENESS IS <u>NOT</u> SAYING WHAT SOMEONE DID WAS OK....IT IS SIMPLY LETTING GO.

2. FORGIVENESS IS <u>NOT</u> AN EMOTION – IT <u>IS</u> A CHOICE

3. ONCE YOU FORGIVE, GOD CAN HEAL THE HURT CAUSED BY THE ACTION YOU ARE FORGIVING.

Forgiveness is not saying what someone did was OK

Let's set our compass for "true north" by digging into God's word. What does He have to say about forgiveness?

Read Isaiah 5:13. How does this verse speak to you?

Many people are ignorant of the consequences of unforgiveness. We are going to check into God's word to see what HE has to say on this.

What does Proverbs 14:12 say about leaning on our own understanding?

I don't know about you, but I certainly don't want to take the wrong path. That means I can't depend upon my emotions or even the things I think I know to guide me in my decisions. So let's dig in…

I love Peter! He certainly doesn't have a pristine reputation; instead, when we think of Peter, the old adage "open mouth – insert foot" comes to mind. However, I love Peter because he wasn't afraid to ask all of those questions many of us would like to ask, but don't want to appear ignorant or foolish. Good old Peter took the fall for us! Let's listen in on one of his conversations with Jesus.

Matt 18:21-22 Then Peter came and said to Him, "Lord, how often shall my brother sin against me and I forgive him? Up to seven times? Jesus said to him, "I do not say to you, up to seven times, but up to seventy times seven."

What was Peter asking from Jesus?

Forgiveness is not a number – it is an attitude

Do you see Peter was asking Jesus for a number so he could fulfill the law concerning forgiveness? Sometimes we are tempted to limit our forgiveness just like Peter was trying to do. Jesus' response to Peter shows that forgiveness is not a number – it is an attitude. We must determine to walk in an attitude of forgiveness before any offense occurs. Then, whenever something happens, our attitude has already been set. We find ourselves forgetting about numbers and extending grace where it is so desperately needed.

If Jesus thought attitude was so important, we'd better check into that further. Let's talk about attitude. When I think of the word attitude, Philippians 2:5 comes to mind. Look it up and write it here.

Forgiveness is a free act of the will towards someone who does not deserve it

I have a precious friend who loves to take detours. She and her husband can be traveling down a highway when she sees a side road and wonders where it would take them. Sometimes it's a dead end, but many times they see things they would have never seen if they stayed on the highway. Let's take a detour today and glean some gems we need to know before we continue down the highway we've been on.

The NASB and NLT use the word attitude; NIV and NKJV use the word mind-set or mind. The next three verses in Philippians 2 explain what the writer is saying. Study them and answer the following question.

What was Jesus' opinion of Himself in verse 6?

What is your opinion of yourself? Jesus knew Who He was. When He was extending forgiveness to us, it wasn't because He thought He deserved to be punished for someone else's sin. Sometimes we think we honor God when we are actually walking in false humility. We wrongly think it is OK to be abused or sinned against. God isn't saying that. He wants us to know who we are so we can see that, like Jesus, forgiveness is a free act of the will towards someone who does not deserve it. In order for that to happen, we need to know the reality of who we are.

Turn to Psalm 139:13-14. Who created you? _____ Was He wise enough

to know what He was doing? _____ What does HE say about

you in verse 14? _____

_____ Do you believe that? _____This verse says

that deep within your soul, you know the truth.

Sometimes life gets in the way and covers up or negates that truth, but it is still there deep within each one of us. We can never have true peace until we clear away the rubbish and uncover the reality of our value. Jesus knew who He was. He didn't walk in false humility. He knew He was equal with His Father. That's who He was and that's who He is. We can't say that, but we CAN SAY what HE says about us. Verse 14 begins with the words, "I will give thanks to You because"…if we truly believe we are an amazing work of art created by our Father Who loves us deeply, we, too will begin by saying "Thank You, Father, because I am fearfully and wonderfully made"

Perfection or relationship - that was the choice God had to make when He began contemplating creating mankind. What was His goal? If it was that man would remain the perfect object that was originally created, there would be no place for choice; however, neither would there be opportunity for relationship. Without a choice, man could continue in perfection, but the relationship would only be one of master and slave. True relationship demands a choice for both parties involved. Because of His deep desire for a genuine non-compulsory relationship with us, God gave up perfection. He knew what it would cost Him. He knew the choice that would one day be made. He knew the only way to redeem us back to the state of perfection…it would cost the life of His Only Begotten Son. Remember in the garden where Jesus said, "if there be any other way"…the fact that no other way was offered tells us there was no other way. So, in spite of the wrong choices, in spite of the cost, God chose relationship. Not only did it cost Him His Son, it cost Him perfection in this lifetime. HE made the choice. He doesn't expect perfection - why should we?

Don't get me wrong…God desires a perfect heart from each one of us. This doesn't offer cheap grace - it offers so much more…value, freedom, destiny. We were created out of God's great love and desire for relationship…not just relationship with mankind, but a relationship with YOU…relationship with ME. That should speak loudly of our value. We aren't submitting to God as puppets who have no choice. We're too valuable for that. We have been given the gift of choice…now God is asking us to do what Jesus did with HIS choice. Before we go back to the highway let's look up one more scripture.

I John 3:1 – What does it say?

What did God lavish upon us? _____ _____

Did He have to do that or was it HIS choice? _____

Do you recognize how this validates our worth? He didn't have to do it. We were so valuable HE CHOSE to lavish His love upon us.

_____

To *choose relationship is to choose forgiveness*

What does HE call us? _____ What is the scripture's

response to that? _____

AND SUCH WE ARE!!! Let's walk in who He created us to be!

Now that we know who we are and how greatly we are loved, we are free to make a serious choice. God chose relationship over perfection. We have the same choice. God couldn't have both and neither can we. Jesus, knowing Who He was, chose to do what was necessary to forgive and give opportunity for reconciliation to you and me…even though we didn't deserve it. There are people in our lives that are imperfect. Sometimes, because of that, they hurt us. They don't deserve to be forgiven. At those times we must ask ourselves which we want…perfection or relationship. We can't have both…to choose relationship is to choose forgiveness. There is no other way. It is the way of love…

Tomorrow we will get back on the highway, but hopefully today you took an amazing detour. Journal how today's lesson has spoken to you. It's good to write it down. Sometimes we find ourselves in a dark spot and need to go back to what we learned to be the truth.

WEEK TWO - FREEDOM THROUGH FORGIVENESS

Did you keep Philippians 2 marked while we were on our detour? Let's turn back and start down that highway again...the good thing is that we have checked our attitude before we begin our trip. But wait...there's more...

Let's take back up with Philippians 2: 7-8. We saw in verse 6 that Jesus was fully aware

of who He was...equal with God, even the very form of God...yet in verses 7 & 8 we

are told He willingly left that form for the form of _____. Having done that...

having been born into the world as a man, and having lived among us, He then humbled Himself even further by taking our sin upon Himself and dying a cruel death on a cross. He did whatever it took for the guilty ones to be reunited to the Father. THIS IS FORGIVENESS IN ACTION.

We stand in total need of the very thing we struggle to grant

My desire is that we develop a clear understanding of forgiveness. Forgiveness is paying the price so that the one who is guilty can go free. **WAIT – THAT'S NOT FAIR!!!** Why should the innocent pay the price for the guilty? I don't know the answer to that, except that I am so thankful for His decision to pay the price I could not pay. Without

forgiveness, neither you nor I would have any chance to spend eternity in heaven in

God's presence. I don't deserve that kind of love. Do you? _____ Our flesh cringes when God asks us to forgive those who have sinned against us, yet we stand in total need of the very thing we struggle to grant. II Timothy 3:16 says God's word is our teacher. Turn to Colossians 2: 13-15 and paraphrase these verses with me.

When you were _____ because of your _____

Christ forgave us _____ our sins. He _____ all

the charges against us by _____ them to _____

_____. He _____ the rulers and authorities; and

_____ over them.

How did God nail our sins to the cross? II Corinthians 5:21 answers that. I like the way the NLT records this, so I am printing it here. "For God made Christ, who never sinned, to be the offering for our sin, so that we could be made right with God through Christ."

Underline the phrase that speaks to whether Christ ever sinned. Circle what He chose to be for us. Place a box around why He did it. Do you see a clear picture of true

forgiveness?_____

WEEK TWO - FREEDOM THROUGH FORGIVENESS

One more verse – Colossians 3:12-13. How does God say WE are to forgive?

_____ _____

What extent did Jesus go to in order to offer total forgiveness? _____

_____ Pretty hard stuff to follow…. this calls for a story.

Remember, I love stories – but so does Jesus. He told them all the time! Let's listen in when He responds with a story as He continues His conversation with Peter in Matthew 18:

Forgiveness is not about being fair

""23 Peter, the kingdom of heaven is like a king who wanted to settle accounts with his servants. 24 As he began the settlement, a man who owed him ten thousand bags of gold was brought to him. 25 Since he was not able to pay, the master ordered that he and his wife and his children and all that he had be sold to repay the debt. 26 At this the servant fell on his knees before him. 'Be patient with me,' he begged, 'and I will pay back everything.' 27 The servant's master took pity on him, canceled the debt and let him go. 28 But when that servant went out, he found one of his fellow servants who owed him a hundred silver coins. He grabbed him and began to choke him. 'Pay back what you owe me!' he demanded. 29 His fellow servant fell to his knees and begged him, 'Be patient with me, and I will pay it back.' 30 But he refused. Instead, he went off and had the man thrown into prison until he could pay the debt. 31 When the other servants saw what had happened, they were outraged and went and told their master everything that had happened. 32 Then the master called the servant in. 'You wicked servant,' he said, 'I canceled all that debt of yours because you begged me to. 33 Shouldn't you have had mercy on your fellow servant just as I had on you?' 34 In anger his master handed him over to the jailers to be tortured, until he should pay back all he owed. 35 THIS IS HOW MY HEAVENLY FATHER WILL TREAT EACH OF YOU UNLESS YOU FORGIVE YOUR BROTHER OR SISTER FROM YOUR HEART.'"

According to verse 24, how much did the servant owe the king? _____

What did the king require the servant to pay? _____ How much

did it cost the king to forgive the servant? _____ Did the servant

deserve to go free? _____ Does that seem fair? _____

Can you see that forgiveness is not about being fair – it is about being willing to let

the offender go free?

How much did the second servant owe the first servant? _____ Was it the same amount the first servant owed the king? _____ Can you see, however, that according to what the servant owned, it would seem like the same amount to him as the 10,000 bags of gold would seem to the king? _____

_____

According to verses 26 and 29, were the requests from the two servants the same or totally different? _____ What were they asking for from the one they owed? _____ _____ Looking at verses 27 and 30, was the king willing to forgive? _____ How about the first servant? _____

_____

FORGIVENESS IS NOT AN EMOTION; IT IS NOT A FEELING; IT IS A CHOICE. IT IS NOT FAIR – IT IS A DETERMINATION TO DO WHATEVER IS NECESSARY, THAT THE ONE WHO "OWES YOU" **AND DOES NOT DESERVE TO GO FREE**, CAN GO FREE. **HOWEVER, FORGIVENESS IS NEVER SAYING THE GUILTY ONE IS NOT GUILTY.**

Who is the king representing to us? _____ Who is the first servant representing? _____ What about the second servant?

_____

What does Verse 35 say God will do if we do not forgive? _____

_____

What are some areas where torturers could be operating in a person's life? _____

_____

_____

Torturers might work in our physical bodies, our emotions, our mind, our relationships, and even in our finances. Whose choice is it whether we entertain the torturers or not? _____ When we have unforgiveness, we open ourselves to satan.

Forgiveness is not an emotion, it is not a feeling, it is a choice

Forgiveness is never saying the guilty one is not guilty

WEEK TWO - FREEDOM THROUGH FORGIVENESS

The Lord's Prayer is familiar to all of us. Most of the time we recite Matthew 6:12 as "forgive us our sins as we forgive those who sin against us". Interestingly, in the KJV, NASB and NIV we read. "And forgive us our debts as we forgive our debtors." Proverbs 22:7 tells us that the debtor is the lender's slave. This takes the story that Jesus was telling in Matthew 18 and puts it into our daily lives…Isn't that just like Him?!!! He tells us our forgiveness/unforgiveness will either set them free or imprison them…so glad He also tells us the personal consequences to our choice!

Remember…He is the author of forgiveness

Tomorrow we will look even closer at what forgiveness looks like, but for today, take time to honestly assess your life. What evidence do you see that might indicate the presence of torturers operating there? Take heart. God only shows these things to set us free. His goal is to liberate you and me in any area that might be an open door for the enemy. His love is like that… remember…He is the author of forgiveness.

Wow...are you finding this forgiveness stuff as challenging as me? Let's start back down that highway by turning to Ephesians 4: 29-32. We may need to turn off the highway again and camp here for the entire day...but if we do, we can count on seeing some beautiful scenery!

Begin by writing verse 29 so we can take a good look at it.

Now, keep your finger there and turn to Matthew 7:3. Write it here.

Do you see where I'm headed? One more scripture. Paraphrase what Ecclesiastes 7: 20-22 tells us.

According to Ephesians 4:29, would you find yourself innocent or guilty of break-ing God's word? _____ If you said "guilty", we are both in the same boat…and in need of forgiveness. Now look a couple of verses down at verse 31. How would you declare yourself according to that scripture – innocent or guilty? _____ If you said "guilty", I would say, "me too"…and in need of forgiveness AGAIN. When we blow it – when we know it's wrong and do it anyway – we need forgiveness. Yet in the Lord's Prayer, we ask God to forgive us as we forgive others. His response to that is that, if we forgive others, God will forgive us; if we do not forgive others, God will not forgive us.(Matthew 6:12-15) Hmmm….lets go on to Ephesians 4:32. Write it here below.

Underline how we are to forgive others.

Aaaah!!!...If we are to do that – if we are to forgive as Christ forgave us – the question must be answered, "How did Christ forgive us? What were His perimeters? Hop into my vehicle and come with me to Ephesians 2: 1-9. I think we can find the answer to our many questions right there. It's a long portion of scripture. I tend to shy away from using that much in one setting, but call it a detour if you would like. We have to stop and see this…

"Once you were dead because of your disobedience and your many sins. You used to live in sin, just like the rest of the world, obeying the devil—the commander of the powers in the unseen world. He is the spirit at work in the hearts of those who refuse to obey God. All of us used to live that way, following the passionate desires and in-clinations of our sinful nature. By our very nature we were subject to God's anger, just like everyone else. But God is so rich in mercy, and He loved us so much, that even though we were dead because of our sins, He gave us life when He raised Christ from the dead. (It is only by God's grace that you have been saved!) For He raised us from the dead along with Christ and seated us with Him in the heavenly realms because we are united with Christ Jesus. So God can point to us in all future ages as examples of the in-credible wealth of His grace and kindness toward us, as shown in all He has done for us who are united with Christ Jesus. God saved you by His grace when you believed. And you can't take credit for this; it is a gift from God. Salvation is not a reward for the good things we have done, so none of us can boast about it. For we are God's masterpiece. He has created us anew in Christ Jesus, so we can do the good things He planned for us long ago." Ephesians 2:1-10 NLT

One final scripture on this. Turn to Colossians 3: 12-13: "…put on a heart of

_____, _____, _____,

_____, and _____, bearing with one

another, and _____ each other, whoever has a complaint against any one;

just as _____forgave you, so also _____. (NASB)

In school I loved True and False questions…I had a 50% chance of being right! Let's see how we fare on this next section:

True or False?

_____ **We deserve to be forgiven.**

_____ **He forgave us anyway.**
(How many times do we say "They don't deserve to be forgiven."? --- Is there someone in your life who "doesn't deserve to be forgiven?")

_____ **We can always find a way to "make it up" to God.**
(Have you ever said, "They can never repay for what they have done."? --- Is there a circumstance in your life that brings that type of response?)

_____ **He waits until we ask before He ever offers forgiveness.**
(Do we offer conditional forgiveness? "If they ask me I'll forgive, but I'm not going to if they don't ask." --- What about it? Are you still holding unforgiveness against someone because they "never asked"?)

_____ **Before we wanted forgiveness, He offered it to us;**
(What is your attitude towards this? Possibly, "They don't even want to be forgiven!" (Since when did that become a prerequisite in God's eyes? This is not about them…it's about our response to God.)

_____ **Before we realized we needed it; it was there.**
(Did I just hear you say, "They don't even know they've done anything wrong."? (That's OK…forgive them anyway.)

FORGIVENESS IS A CHOICE; IT IS NOT AN EMOTION; IT IS NOT SAYING WHAT THE OTHER PERSON DID WAS OK.

Think about those people in your lives. If you feel comfortable, list them below (or you might put their initials). Determine to get back on the highway of forgiveness. You will be amazed at how the scenery is changed!

This is a rather short but intense day. Tomorrow we will look at some other benefits of forgiveness. For today, be blessed of the Lord as you model His Word. **...God reconciled us to Himself and gave us the ministry of reconciliation...He has committed to us the word of reconciliation. 2 Corinthians 5:18-19**

God reconciled us to Himself and gave us the ministry of reconciliation

WEEK TWO - FREEDOM THROUGH FORGIVENESS

It's story time again…we're going to look at another day in the life of Jesus…should be interesting and insightful…

Mark 11:12-14 "And on the next day, when they had departed from Bethany, He became hungry. And seeing at a distance a fig tree in leaf, He went to see if perhaps He would find anything on it; and when He came to it, He found nothing but leaves, for it was not the season for figs. And He answered and said to it, "May no one ever eat fruit from you again!" And His disciples were listening." (His disciples were listening… smart guys!)

Mark 11: 20-25 "And as they were passing by in the morning, they saw the fig tree withered from the roots up. And being reminded, Peter said to Him, Rabbi, behold the fig tree which You cursed has withered." And Jesus answered saying to them, "Have faith in God. Truly I say to you, whoever says to this mountain, 'Be taken up and cast into the sea, and does not doubt in his heart, but believes that what he says is going to happen; it shall be granted him. Therefore, I say to you, all things for which you pray and ask, believe that you have received them, and they shall be granted you. 25) And whenever you stand praying, forgive, if you have anything against anyone; so that your Father also who is in heaven may forgive you your transgressions."

Jesus dealt with the root issue

What happened to the fig tree that Jesus cursed? (verse 20)

_____ Jesus dealt with the **root issue**, and the entire

plant withered. That's the concept that God uses when He deals with issues in our lives. He goes to the core issue and when that is taken care of, the symptoms wither and die.

Who does Jesus tell that they can speak to the mountains and the mountains must

obey? _____ Find John 8: 31 and write what Jesus told those

who believed in Him.. _____

_____ How can we become

His disciples? _____ _____

Ask yourself honestly, would Jesus consider you one of His disciples? A disciple obeys His master. If you desire to be His disciple, what does verse 25 say in the scripture I printed above?

WEEK TWO - FREEDOM THROUGH FORGIVENESS

Are there possibly some mountains in your life that refuse to budge because you haven't finished reading that last verse in the story? We can speak to the mountain all day long, and it will simply smile and remain standing if we are walking in unforgiveness… another benefit of "listening to the Master" and obeying what He says.

We can speak to the mountain all day long, and it will simply smile and remain standing if we are walking in unforgiveness

Read Isaiah 59:1, 2 "Behold the Lord's _____ is not so short that it cannot save; neither is His _____ so dull that it cannot hear. But your _____ have made a separation between you and your God, and your _____ have hid His face from you, so that He does not hear."

Is Unforgiveness a sin? _____ Do you see that Unforgiveness can keep our prayers from being fully answered? _____

Heb 12:15 "See to it that no one comes short of the grace of God, that no root of _____ springing up cause trouble, and by it many be defiled." According to this verse, what does bitterness do? _____

This tells us someone can actually come short of the grace of God because of bitterness in YOUR heart towards them? Again, our choice – we can be a life-giver or a bitter, cruel defiler of those around us. (Hmmm…I smell something…is it a sweet smell coming from your countenance…or something that needs worked on?)

In 2 Corinthians 2:10-11 Paul says, "But one whom you forgive anything, I forgive also; for indeed what I have forgiven, …I did it for your sakes in the presence of Christ, so that no advantage would be taken of us by Satan, for we are not ignorant of his _____" . Unforgiveness gives satan an _____.

It is actually an open door. Who is responsible for opening that door? _____

OUCH! That would be me!!! Better shut that door really quickly…

Matthew 18:18-19 "Truly I say to you, whatever you bind on earth shall have been bound in heaven; and whatever you loose on earth shall have been loosed in heaven. Again I say to you, that if two of you agree on earth about anything that they may ask, it shall be done for them by My Father who is in heaven." Whatever _____ bind on earth is bound in heaven. Who has the power to bind or set free? _____.

In our story yesterday we saw that the king had the power to imprison the one who owed him. Think about it…is there someone in your life that needs to be set free?

Look up Psalm 37:8 and write it here.

Underline the three things God asks us to stop doing. What does He say will happen if we continue doing these things? _____

Once we get on that slippery slope, it can go downhill pretty fast.

This is getting a little intense. Perhaps it's time for another story break…hopefully this will add some needed perspective to forgiveness…

It was such a simple statement – that's how profound truths are often delivered…so simple, yet so profound. She didn't even realize the depth of her words…she simply spoke them, and then went on…but me – I was locked there. All day I thought about those words. Even the next day and the next…and here I am, four days later, still rehearsing her words. She spoke about judgment, even though she didn't have a clue that she was quoting Romans 2:1, 2 ""Therefore you are without excuse, every man of you who passes judgment, for in that you judge another, you condemn yourself…And we know that the judgment of God rightly falls upon those who practice such things."

WEEK TWO - FREEDOM THROUGH FORGIVENESS

o simply said…"Someone can do you good day after day…day after day they say good things, do good things, are a blessing to you. Then one day they do something wrong – maybe it's their words, or their actions, but it was wrong. What happens to all of the good things they did? You separate that person from all the good things they did and lock them into the thing they did wrong. In your eyes you make them become that evil person who always does wrong. That one thing defines them from that day on."… I couldn't get away from those words. It was about forgiveness, but it went much farther and so much deeper than forgiveness would go. Forgiveness is letting go of an offense; this, however, places yourself as God in deciding the value of another human being. How many times have I allowed one or two character flaws to define a person, all the while desiring to have mercy and grace extended to me in my own weaknesses? God's Word says there is only one God – and it isn't me. It's HIM. Could it be that the problem actually lies within me…not the other person? Please forgive me, Father, and infuse me with love, mercy and grace for others…and thank you that, if I will give it to others, I will receive those same blessings in return – pressed down, shaken together and running over. Indeed, You are such a merciful, good God. I would rather be judged by You than by me.

How many times have I allowed one or two character flaws to define a person

I think I'll have a cup of forgiveness…how about you?

Look up Luke 6:36-38. Write the last sentence of verse 38.

In the first sentence of verse 38, to what degree will you receive back what you give

to others? _____

If you judge, you will _____;

If you condemn, you will _____;

If you forgive, you will _____.

What a wonderful story…what a wonderful choice… and just think…running over…I think I'll have a cup of forgiveness…how about you?

WEEK TWO - FREEDOM THROUGH FORGIVENESS

James was quite a guy…He wasn't into mincing words. He begins his book in the New Testament by getting right to the point. God is into molding you into the image of His Son…so get on with it!!! Consider it joy when God is working on you through various trials; if you need to know something, ask God; don't fall into the lie that God would be tempting you or leading you into evil; and watch that tongue!!! Let's see what else James has to say. I think we need to listen to this fellow…

James 1: 22-24. It would be good for us to write out verse 22.

God is into molding you into the image of His Son…so get on with it!!!

We've heard what God has said about forgiveness…the truth and the consequences. Now we need to ask ourselves if we are just going to be hearers only, or if we are going to actually do what He is telling us.

One more scripture passage before we get started. Look at Luke 6: 46-49.

"Why do you call Me, 'Lord, Lord,' and do not _____?

Everyone who comes to Me and hears My words and _____

is like a man building a house, who dug deep and laid a foundation _____

_____;

The one who has heard and has NOT acted accordingly, is like a man who built a

house on the ground _____

Did their foundation determine whether a storm would hit their lives? _____

What was the difference that the foundation made?_____

_____

_____

If you call Jesus "Lord", what are you going to do with what you just learned about

forgiveness? _____

God doesn't need your feelings. He only needs your willingness to forgive

Today's lesson is pretty simple. We are going to put into action what we have learned this week. Get alone with God and ask Him to bring to mind anyone you need to forgive…Little and big things alike. Phil 4:13 – ("I can do all things through Christ Who strengthens me.") You can forgive everyone through Christ! You can't depend on your feelings. God doesn't need your feelings. He only needs your willingness to forgive.

Forgiveness is not passive. You can't just let the situation slip by until you think you've forgotten it. It goes INWARD instead of leaving. You have to look at that situation and CHOOSE to forgive. It may be a person, God (even though God is perfect, sometimes we hold unforgiveness towards Him because He didn't answer our prayers like we wanted, or in the timeline we thought He should), or even yourself! (who are you to say you shouldn't be forgiven when God says He will forgive anyone who asks?)

Forgiveness is not passive

Once you have forgiven, ask God to bring healing into your life in that area.

Happy forgiving!!!

FREEDOM FROM UNCONFESSED SIN

Unconfessed sin is simply sin that you refuse to call sin. This doesn't mean you have to go back to birth and ask forgiveness for every sin you committed by name. It means that when God shows you that something in your life is sin, you admit it as sin, repent, and accept forgiveness and cleansing for it.

2 Timothy 2: 20-22 If we _____ ourselves, we will be a vessel of _____

1 John 1: 5-10 If we say we have no sin, we are only _____ ourselves and

not living in the _____.

If we _____ our sins to God, He is _____ and just to

_____ us our sins and to _____ us from all

unrighteousness.

Galatians 5:19-21 Sin can be an _____ or an

_____.

Jeremiah 5:21-25 God will not share the honor of being _____

with _____ or _____

Psalms 107:17-21 God sent His _____ and healed them, and

_____ them from their destructions.

Psalms 32:1-5 When I _____ my sins, God forgives my _____

51

WEEK THREE - FREEDOM FROM UNCONFESSED SIN

ONLY REPENTANCE CAN FREE US FROM GUILT.

Proverbs 1:23 If we listen to God's reproof, He will bring

_____ of His word to us.

Psalms 69:5, 6 May those who seek You not be dishonored through me,
O God of Israel.

John 3:20 All who do evil _____ the light for fear their

_____ will be exposed.

Our prayer should be Psalm 19:14:

May the _____ of my mouth, and the meditation of my

_____ be pleasing to you, O LORD, my rock and redeemer.

Psalms 51:10-13 Create in me a _____ heart, O God. Renew a

_____ spirit within me…..Make me _____ to obey You.

Ask God to reveal to you any unconfessed sin in your life. Then confess it and accept forgiveness and cleansing for it according to I John 1:9. Ask God to continue revealing unconfessed sin in your life in order that you may be free.

NOTES:

WEEK THREE - FREEDOM FROM UNCONFESSED SIN

I certainly didn't have time for a detour this morning…but then, that's when many of those detours occur, don't they? I decided to make muffins for some friends who are coming over. I didn't want to bother getting out my large mixer, so decided to use my favorite old fashioned pastry blender – the kind used to cut butter into your biscuit dough. I was excited to try this new recipe, so hurriedly added all the ingredients together and started blending. Admittedly, it had been awhile since I had used this particular utensil (actually it had been awhile since I had done that thing called baking). I didn't even think about a maintenance check…after all, it was just a pastry blender. However, just when I had the blending rhythm going just right - BAMM!!! The nut holding the handle of the blender flew off, and batter went everywhere; however, the worst part was I couldn't find the nut!!! I searched high and low with no nut in sight. I even donned gloves and, spoonful by spoonful, checked the mixing bowl… nothing. It wasn't on the floor, on my range beside the counter, in the sink…nowhere to be found…only batter splattered everywhere…including all over my precious microwave. What a mess!!!

I have to tell you…I love my microwave! I love it so much that I dote on it. It is ALWAYS clean. No matter what the rest of my house looks like, 99.99% of the time… if you come to my home, and make your way through my latest projects…if you reach my beloved (yet small) microwave and open the door, you will be amazed! It is spotless!!! ALWAYS!!! I was so sad as I took my dishcloth and lovingly cleaned the batter spewed on my prize possession. Then the thought came…maybe the nut was under the microwave…let me check.

When I moved my beloved, beautifully clean microwave out from the counter wall, I was horrified. UGGH! My precious microwave was sitting on a mound of dust and dirt – it would take the big guns to clean this mess!!! HOW DID ALL THAT DIRT GET THERE??!? How could I not have noticed??? I mean, really…how did that happen?…then reality hit me that all that dirt had collected one spec at a time, undetected, and allowed to accumulate through neglect.

Hmmm…so was the detour really about a broken kitchen utensil, or was it a lesson I needed to learn? The thought struck me… sin is like that as well. Yes, sometimes there are big things that happen that we readily take care of (like the batter spewed all over the counter)…but many times, it's just those little things…things so easily undetected…that begin to accumulate…and one day the "dirt pile" is pretty high, and we're not sure how it got there.

We may not see our "dirt pile" of sin, but God knows it's there. He is so loving…loves us just where we are, but loves us way too much to leave us there. Let's see what His Word says about our sin…and His Love.

Many times, those little things begin to accumulate…and one day the "dirt pile" is pretty high, and we're not sure how it got there.

God loves us just where we are, but loves us way too much to leave us there.

WEEK THREE - FREEDOM FROM UNCONFESSED SIN

Read Hebrews 12: 5-11 and answer the questions below:

Write out verse 5

This verse speaks of both sides of discipline. Neither are we to take this discipline lightly, nor are we to faint under it. Underline the two ways we are to respond to God's discipline.

Verse 6 tells us why we need to both listen, and yet not be downcast. According to that verse, why does God discipline us?

Verse 10 adds to that. What is God trying to work into our lives through His discipline?

Finally, in verse 11, what does God say will be the result of that discipline?

God knows that the dirt in our lives, many times accumulated little by little over a considerable period of time, will dull our senses and cause us to lose sight of the joy and peace that comes from a clean heart. Sometimes, in His love, He takes us on a detour so we can see things we've missed…sometimes, we need to look from a different viewpoint to gain a clearer perspective. We can find that perspective in Isaiah 59:1-2. Write it here.

What does it say in verse 1 about God's power to hear and answer our prayers?

Looking at verse two, what is the real problem, and who is at fault?

The next 13 verses are a sad indictment for those who continue in unconfessed sin. However, verses 16-21 show us once again of God's relentless love for us. Even when we go astray, God says He will save us with His own mighty arm. Verse 17 reads, "And He put on righteousness like a breastplate, and a helmet of salvation on His head;… hmmm…reminds me of our earlier study of Ephesians 6:14-17. God, Who knows the weapons that are successful against the enemy, not only uses them Himself, but gives them to us as a gift. II Corinthians 10:4 says God has given us weapons that are divinely powerful for the destruction of fortresses. One of those weapons is humility to recognize and confess our sins.

I love my pastry blender. It's an old friend. It's always been faithful…well, most of the time. Occasionally, it does what it did this morning, but I've always been able to locate the nut and screw it back on. But now…what am I going to do with this old friend that let me down? Can I ever trust it again? Do I discard it, or do I make an allowance for this one fault it has? It would require me checking to make sure the nut is on right each time I use it. Is it worth it? (sigh…)

So…what about us? We love God, and we truly want to obey Him…well, most of the time. Occasionally, we really mess up…I mean we can cause a pretty stinky mess (can I get an Amen?). God could just toss us to the side and say we're not worth keeping… and He would actually be right…we aren't. But that's where HIS love and grace comes in big time. Look up Romans 5: 6 and write it here.

What does God call us at that point?

Now look up Eph 2:5 and write it here.

One of those weapons is humility to recognize and confess our sins

WEEK THREE - FREEDOM FROM UNCONFESSED SIN

In spite of our ungodly status, what did He display that allowed us to be saved? Law or

grace? _____ Condemnation or love? _____

We first need to see that God isn't mad at us. He sees all the dirt and broken, unstable pieces in our lives, but willingly pours out His love and grace upon us...forever changing our status from unworthy to exquisitely valuable. That lets us know that when He points out something that is out of sync in our lives (that would be sin), He isn't doing it to condemn us, but to set us free.

He sees all the dirt and broken, unstable pieces in our lives, but willingly pours out His love and grace upon us...forever changing our status from unworthy to exquisitely valuable.

Check out Psalm 32: 1-5 What does He call us when our sins are forgiven?

What does He say about us when we try to hide our sin?

What does verse 5 say God will do if we confess our sins to Him?

The real danger is that it can start accumulating until we find ourselves doing things we never thought we would ever do... taking us places we never dreamed we would go.

Many translations use the word "guilt". Have you ever felt guilty?

Is there something currently in your life that you need to stop right now and confess to Him? You see, He already knows it...no hiding it from God...but when we try, we are miserable. The real danger is that it can start accumulating until we find ourselves doing things we never thought we would ever do...taking us places we never dreamed we would go. Let's take some time out right now and get serious with God. And in the future, when He takes you on another detour, remember...it's worth the time to stop and listen. When God speaks to our heart, we need to listen and respond. "And He forgave the guilt of my sin"...what a God!!!

WEEK THREE - FREEDOM FROM UNCONFESSED SIN

I love it when my house is clean…when I walk in and everything is in its proper place…all the shelves are dusted and the carpet freshly vacuumed…aaah…I can breathe deeply …everything is right with the world. I tell myself this is good…I'm going to make a daily habit of keeping it this way…after all, how hard could that possibly be? (Yeah, right!!!) The trouble is that life just gets in the way. I hate to admit it, but that happens pretty often. As much as I love a spotless house, I evidently love other things much more.

That also plays out in my spiritual life from time to time. I get so busy with "life" that I forget about the Life-Giver. I pass by my bible on my way out the door…throw up an arrow prayer here and there throughout the day…reason with myself as I climb into bed, that surely God wants me to stay healthy by getting a good night's sleep…have you ever been there? Pretty soon my spiritual life looks like my neglected house… pretty dusty and cluttered. At that point in time, I have to take stock and ask myself, "What would God have to say about this in His word?" We've looked at these scriptures before, but it is worth looking them up again. Let's turn to John 8:31-32 and write it here.

When "busy" goes too far, it can quietly (or not so quietly) become luke-warm…and then cold towards anything that gets in the way of "busy"… even God.

Am I content with my life the way it is?

We'll come back to this scripture, but before we look any deeper, we need to ask ourselves a question: "Am I content with my life the way it is? Do I really want to change anything?" I know some people who are really content with messy houses. They are comfortable just the way they are. Messy is ok…as long as it doesn't get to the point of filthy…but there is a fine line of how long you let "messy" have its way, before it turns the corner. Busy is ok, too. Sometimes it's necessary for a season…but just like "messy", when "busy" goes too far, it can quietly (or not so quietly) become lukewarm…and then cold towards anything that gets in the way of "busy"…even God.

Looking back at the scripture above, what does it say we need to do if we desire to be a disciple of Jesus? A simple definition of disciple is "one who is taught or trained". That sounds like there is some work involved…the question that must be answered is, "is it worth the work"? I'm pretty sure you wouldn't be on Week Three if you were not serious about following Jesus. So what does verse 31 say we must do in order to become

a disciple of Jesus? _____ If we do that, verse 32 promises us

we will _____ and the truth will _____.

What that tells me is that there are some areas in my life that may stay hidden…some

sinful ways I don't recognize…unless I see the truth about my condition. Only when I recognize the truth am I then able to confess that sin in order to be forgiven and cleansed.

Week Three - Freedom From Unconfessed Sin

Let's add II Timothy 3:16 to our list of scriptures to look up. If we remain in God's Word

what are the four benefits listed in this verse?

_____, _____,

_____ and _____.

As we are diligent to read the Word, it will be faithful to point out any "unclean" areas in our lives. Through the previous scriptures, we are now aware of the danger in leaving those spiritual dust balls unattended.

As we are diligent to read the Word, it will be faithful to point out any "unclean" areas in our lives.

God is such a good, loving, gracious Father. He wants to make sure we get this "Truth Thing" right. When Jesus was preparing to leave His disciples, He gave them some comforting words. He promised He would never leave or forsake them. In John 14: 16-17, Jesus tells them the Father will send the Holy Spirit, who will be their Helper. He calls Him the Spirit of Truth. What does He say about the Holy Spirit in John 16:13?

The choice is ours…and God will honor that choice.

Now turn to John 14:26 (NIV) and fill in the blanks. "But the Helper, the Holy Spirit, whom the Father will send in My name, will teach you _____

_____, and will _____ _____ of everything I have said to

you." When we hear the word, "remind", we recognize that, in order for us to be reminded, we must have already heard it before. If we have neglected to spend time reading God's Word, there will be nothing for the Holy Spirit to remind us of. We, then, have a responsibility to do our part. Look at II Chronicles 16:9 and write just the first sentence of that verse here.

What does God desire to do? _____

Who is He looking for in order to do that? _____

_____

Whether or not God can accomplish HIS part – HIS desire – depends upon whether we place Him first in our lives. That means some things in our life might have to go…some things that were at the forefront may have to take a back seat if we are really serious about our walk with God. Deuteronomy 30:19 tells us the choice is ours…and God will honor that choice.

WEEK THREE - FREEDOM FROM UNCONFESSED SIN

So what does all of this have to do with unconfessed sin?...How is this relevant to our lesson today? To answer that, I will go back to the story about my microwave. Because I wasn't aware of the dust and dirt accumulating behind it…because it remained unseen…it was able to build up until it was a major task to get all of the dirt and grime cleaned from the counter. Without a consistent dose of God's Word and the empowerment of the Holy Spirit to reveal necessary truths to us, we are left at the mercy of our own understanding or physical eyes…which is powerless against an unseen enemy operating in heavenly places. Proverbs 14: 12 gives us a stern warning. "There is a

_____ that _____ _____ to a man, but its end is the way of

_____. YIKES!!! Let's stay away from that erroneous way. Instead, Psalm 139:23-24 seems to offer the better way. Write it here:

Without a consistent dose of God's Word and the empowerment of the Holy Spirit to reveal necessary truths to us, we are left at the mercy of our own understanding or physical eyes

Today, once again, please take time to ask God to reveal any hidden sin in your life. It may be just a small dust ball – it may be something that has already put its roots down. Either way, God promises in I John 1:9 that, if we confess our sin, He will be faithful and just to forgive us, and cleanse us from all unrighteousness. As we continue in this series, we will become more aware of other things that trip us up. However, let's not wait to deal with anything the Lord wants to show us today. Happy cleaning!

WEEK THREE - FREEDOM FROM UNCONFESSED SIN

Since our heart is so important to God, (2 Chronicles 16:9), we'd better make sure it is in the right spot. Let's start in Job 22:21-30 (NASB). There is much treasure to be mined from these verses. Treat them as though you are mining for gold.
Write verses 21-22 here:

We will never be at peace with God as long as we want our own way.

What does verse 21 say we must do to be at peace with God? _____.

We will never be at peace with God as long as we want our own way. Circle where verse 22 says we are to establish God's Word.

Verses 23-27 (NASB) blend together to give step by step instructions on what surrender looks like. Fill in the blanks and watch the plan come together.

1.) _____ to the Almighty;

2.) _____ unrighteousness far from your tent;

3.) _____ YOUR _____ in the dust.

4.) Then the _____ will be your _____.

5.) Then you will _____ in the _____, and

6.) _____ your face to _____.

7.) You will _____ to Him and

8.) He will _____ you.

Look back over those verses. Do you want God to hear you when you pray? This is step by step instructions on how to reach that goal. BUT WAIT…once that goal is reached, there are some amazing benefits. When you are truly seeking God and listening for His voice…when He is your gold, verse 28 comes into play. Write it here:

It is a very dangerous thing to simply decree the things we want, when we have not submitted our desires (gold) to God first.

Too often we hear this verse taken out of context. It is a very dangerous thing to simply decree the things we want, when we have not submitted our desires (gold) to God first. However, once we have laid it down, we have the opportunity to partner with God, using our words to bring His will into our circumstances. Look back over that verse again, and capture the power God gives His servant whose heart is wholly His.

Verse 29 says that once we have decreed God's will, even if the enemy comes against us, we can be confident that God is moving. Then, just look at verse 30…what a powerful verse!!! Write it so you get the full benefit of it:

We have the opportunity to partner with God, using our words to bring His will into our circumstances.

Because of the cleanness of YOUR hands (because you have laid your gold in the dust and submitted to God), He will deliver even one who is NOT innocent. Think about that…in fact, think about it over and over again. It should compel us to walk in holiness before God in order that we can be used to advance His Kingdom. What a promise!!!…What a God!!!

Have you ever tackled a project and, just when you stepped back to admire the completed work, you saw one area you had totally missed? That's what I did with this week's lessons. I had "finished" our discussion questions and was ready to move on, when the Holy Spirit stopped me abruptly…"what does confessing sin really look like? Shouldn't everyone have a guide to refer back to in the future?"

I remember hearing oh so many good, powerful sermons! Well…actually I remember that the sermons were really good, and while listening to them, I told myself I needed to remember to walk in the truth I just learned. Unfortunately, by Tuesday afternoon, I couldn't remember what it was that I was so passionate about on Sunday morning. However, IF I had taken notes, I could look back to refresh my memory. Just that simple tool made all the difference. Once I saw the notes, I would remember many of the main points spoken that day.

That is the goal of this lesson. My desire is that it will serve the same purpose as good note taking. We are going to walk through steps of true repentance. Keep these notes handy. Our lives tend to need spring cleaned from time to time.

Our lives tend to need spring cleaned from time to time.

We'll begin with a couple of reminders from Psalm 139. Write verse 1 below.

Read verses 2-4 and record some of the things God knows about us.

Verses 13 & 14 tell us some important truths. Write them in your own words.

As we realize it is God who created us, and intimately knows everything about us, it is wisdom that He is the one we ask to search our hearts. Write verses 23 & 24 here.

Now turn to James 1:5. What happens when we ask God for wisdom?

If we are really serious when we ask God to show us any sin hidden in our heart, He will lovingly answer.

If we are really serious when we ask God to show us any sin hidden in our heart, He will lovingly answer. Once He has done so, the next step is found in James 4:7-10.

"Submit therefore to God. Resist the devil and he will flee from you. **Draw near to God** and He will draw near to you. **Cleanse your hands**, you sinners; and **purify your hearts**, you double-minded. **Be miserable** and **mourn** and **weep**; let your laughter be turned into mourning and your joy to gloom. **Humble yourselves** in the presence of the Lord, and He will exalt you."

God wants to know that we are truly repentant...not just throwing words at him to make us feel better.

What is the first thing we are required to do? _____.

Submitting to someone means we yield to the authority of another; to defer to another's judgment or decision. We see here, that Someone is God. Only after we do that, can we successfully resist the devil and have him flee.

Let's see what submitting to God looks like. What is God asking us to do here? Look back at the scripture and underline the steps He is asking us to take. I have them in bold to help guide you.

As we draw near to Him, we are able to hear when God speaks. Cleansing our hands requires us to be willing to stop doing what we are currently doing that causes our hands to be dirty with sin. It is the first step in being willing to purify our hearts. **GOD WANTS TO KNOW THAT WE ARE TRULY REPENTANT...NOT JUST THROWING WORDS AT HIM TO MAKE <u>US</u> FEEL BETTER.** That's why He says we are to be miserable, and weep and mourn over what we have done. Humbling ourselves means we give up our independence, power, or will, when it is in direct contradiction to God.

WEEK THREE - FREEDOM FROM UNCONFESSED SIN

Once we have truly repented, 2Corinthians 7:9-10 contain our next guidelines.

"I now rejoice, not that you were made sorrowful, but that you were made sorrowful to the point of repentance; for you were made sorrowful according to the will of God, in order that you might not suffer loss in anything through us. For the sorrow that is according to the will of God produces a repentance without regret, leading to salvation; but the sorrow of the world produces death."

When we have become sorrowful to the point of repentance, our sorrow was according to the will of God. Underline that phrase.

What was God's goal in that? (In order that you_____ _____

_____

God is not an angry God, but is always in search of His children's good. He knows the consequences of sin, and desires that we would escape what He calls "suffering loss".

Instead, what does He say "sorrow according to His will" produces? _____

_____. What does it lead to? _____

One of the key phrases in the above scripture is WITHOUT REGRET. Let's look closer at that. Find I John 1:9 and write it here.

What two things does God say He will do if we confess our sins?

_____   _____

Once we TRULY repent and confess it to God, He says he FORGIVES and CLEANSES us. His desire is that we walk in that forgiveness.

Psalm 32:5 (NASB) tells us "I acknowledged my sin to Thee, and my iniquity I did not hide; I said, "I will confess my transgressions to the Lord"; and Thou didst forgive the **guilt** of my sin."

What does it say God forgave? _____

If God forgave our guilt, should we still carry it or should we lay it down?

_____

Which decision would please God? _____

65

WEEK THREE - FREEDOM FROM UNCONFESSED SIN

As we look back at the last sentence of 2 Corinthians 7:10, it states that the sorrow of the world produces death. Our enemy wants us to be sorrowful over our sins. He wants us to weep and mourn every day…however; he wants us to simply continue in that deadly cycle. He comes alongside to condemn and destroy, trying to make sure we never accept the forgiveness, lay the regret down, and walk in newness of life. As long as we are looking inward, we will always see sinful things we have done. All of us are in the same boat. It is only as we look up, and see the finished work of the cross… everything that Jesus did to purchase forgiveness for you and me…only when we receive that finished work – receive that forgiveness – will we ever be able to walk in the resurrection life that God has, in His love, made available for us. It does not please Him when we continue in our sorrow and guilt; instead, it gives Him great joy when we embrace all that His Son accomplished for us. It makes His death worthwhile.

It *gives Him great joy when we embrace all that His Son accomplished for us.*

Ephesians 4: 22-24 is a good guideline for us. "That in reference to your former manner of life, you lay aside the old self, which is being corrupted in accordance with the lusts of deceit, and that you be renewed in the spirit of your mind, and put on the new self, which in the likeness of God has been created in righteousness and holiness of the truth.

What does it say we are to lay down? _____

What needs to be renewed in order to put on the new self? _____

The *old you or the new you…take it from me…new looks good on you*

The Lord keeps bringing us back to the truth that everything hinges on what we allow to dwell in our minds. Remember, it is our choice. Only we can make that choice. God implores us in Deuteronomy 30: 19 to choose life. The old you or the new you…take it from me…new looks good on you.

A QUICK RECAP:

STEP ONE – SUBMIT TO GOD.
STEP TWO – TRULY SORROW OVER OUR SIN.
STEP THREE – REPENT AND ASK FORGIVENESS.
STEP FOUR – RECEIVE THE FORGIVENESS.
STEP FIVE – RECEIVE THE CLEANSING.
STEP SIX – LAY DOWN THE REGRET.
STEP SEVEN -WALK IN THE ABUNDANT FREEDOM THAT FORGIVNESS OFFERS

GALATIONS 5:1 – *"IT IS FOR FREEDOM THAT CHRIST SET US FREE; THEREFORE KEEP STANDING FIRM AND DO NOT BE SUBJECT AGAIN TO A YOKE OF SLAVERY."*

….So glad He reminded me of one more thing…so glad I listened…I love His voice…it leads to LIFE…

Use tomorrow to continue allowing the Lord to show you anything that might stand between where you are, and where He desires to take you. I promise you…itwould only be for your good...

FREEDOM FROM UNBELIEF

NOT BELIEVING IN GOD'S WILLINGNESS, ABILITY AND FAITHFULNESS TO PERFORM HIS WORD

HEBREWS 3:12 - 4:2 Unbelief _____ us from entering God's rest.

HEBREWS 6:9-12 Through _____ & _____

we inherit the promises.

MATTHEW 13:54-58 _____ prevents God from working.

MATTHEW 8:5-13 The _____ realm and _____

realm operate on the same principles.

MATTHEW 9:27-29 Past _____ cannot dictate what God can do.

MATTHEW 14:25-31 Don't allow _____ to determine what

is possible.

MATTHEW 15:22-28 The Canaanite woman was willing to _____

what the Jews were throwing away.

WEEK 4 - FREEDOM FROM UNBELIEF

MARK 9:17-25 When we are _____ with God, He _____ us.

JOHN 20:24-29 Thomas was _____ to accept what he could not see

ROMANS 4:18-22 Faith is an act of choosing to believe God and His Word over the

_____

_____

FAITH IS THE DECISION TO BELIEVE GOD MEANS WHAT HE SAYS.

I JOHN 1:9 Unbelief is a sin and can be confessed, forgiven, and cleansed.

Ask God to reveal His Word in such a way to you personally, that faith in Him will grow until it is a well of living water, springing up inside of you.

NOTES:

I'm learning to appreciate detours. We have an opportunity to see things we would never notice otherwise. Let's go on one today…in fact, let's take a couple. We just might find some nuggets we want to put in our pocket and take back with us. I have a destination in mind, but the destination will certainly be enhanced by these two little side trips.

The fun thing about stories is that our imagination can take us anywhere. I've never been to Israel, but that's where we are headed. Let's pretend it is the Saturday before Easter morning. Take a walk with me to the resurrection site, and let's look at the stone together. We have the benefit of knowing what happens on Easter morning, but for right now, I'm asking you to put that knowledge aside. Take a good look at the stone in front of the tomb. In Mark 16: 3, as three women were on their way to anoint the body of Jesus, they were troubled about something. Write the verse here.

There would never be a stone large enough to triumph over God's power.

Hmmm…must have been a pretty large stone for three women to not be able to move it, yet we know that the next morning, it had been rolled away. Let me ask you this question: "How big would that stone have to be for God to be unable to roll it away? What kind of rock, and what size would be beyond God's capability?" Please don't give me a quick answer. Think about it for awhile. The stone was large enough to cover the entrance of a cave that allowed men to carry a body inside, and lay it on the prepared place. What if it had been three times as big…ten times…one hundred times…would

it have been too big? _____

WEEK 4 - FREEDOM FROM UNBELIEF

Of course, the answer is that it doesn't really matter how big the stone was. There would never be a stone large enough to triumph over God's power. So, let's take another side trip. This time we're going to go even further back in time. I love reading about Joshua...again, we have the vantage point of knowing the "rest of the story". Joshua was simply walking it out. I feel for Joshua...how many of you are like me? I have a personality that likes to know the end of the story, whether it is an actual story, movie, or a football or basketball game. If I know the outcome, I can sit back and enjoy the journey...I can't imagine being Joshua, standing and looking at those walls. Let's go to chapter 6 of the story where Jericho is tightly shut up - no one went out, and no one came in...no getting into that place! Take a moment to turn to Joshua 6 and read the story for yourself. God tells Joshua a really wild, weird story. He tells him if he will just have everyone circle the city once every day for six days, then seven times on the seventh day, finalized by the priest blowing a horn, and the people shouting...the walls are going to fall down flat. Really!!! Common sense would tell us we need to go look at those walls. How strong are they, that God is simply going to lay them flat with a little noise (and obedience) on our part? Joshua 2:15 tells us Rahab's house was on the wall. That would signify the wall had to be pretty wide. I'm not an expert, but Wikipedia.org tells me the wall was approximately 7 feet wide and 17 feet high. There was a 27 feet wide by 9 feet deep ditch surrounding it...no possibility of getting very close. Pretty massive looking structure! So, my question again is this: "How big, how wide...what would the walls need to be made of, and how would they need to be constructed, in order to defy God's power in bringing them down?"

What would the walls need to be made of, and how would they need to be constructed, in order to defy God's power in bringing them down?

"How big do the circumstances in your life need to be, in order for God not to be able to bring order out of chaos, hope from despair, freedom from bondage?"

Again, the answer is clear that the size, weight, or materials have no bearing on the outcome. There is absolutely nothing that is impossible for God...which leads me to the biggest question of all..."How big do the circumstances in your life need to be, in order for God not to be able to bring order out of chaos, hope from despair, freedom from bondage?"...and the list goes on. This detour was not without purpose. It was meant to remind us that the women didn't need to look at the stone...it was rolled away before they ever arrived. Joshua didn't need to consider the size and strength of

the wall. All God asked him to do, was to walk in obedience and watch the walls fall.

What is God asking of you today? _____

_____ Joshua could have looked at the seemingly

insurmountable circumstance and walked away...but he would have denied the entire nation of Israel a clear victory that could only be accredited to an Almighty God.

The real question is this: "Is your life about you, or about what God wants to do in you and through you?" If it's about you, then you would be wise to take the safe, easy road. You will be walking in your own power, so beware...make sure every battle you face is one you can win on your own. If, on the other hand, life is about what God so earnestly desires to do in and through you and me...**WATCH OUT WALLS OF JERICHO...YOU ARE COMING DOWN!!!!!!!**

WEEK 4 - FREEDOM FROM UNBELIEF

To fight the battle God's way, we need to put on some armor. Let's begin with the Sword of the Spirit – God's Word. Look up Romans 10: 17 and write it below:

The text is speaking of faith in God. **Hearing the word of God produces faith in the hearer.** Let me insert here, that you hear every word you speak…hmmm…just saying. We need to be careful what we speak. If hearing God's Word produces faith in God, let's see what hearing from the world produces. Ephesians 4:17-18 (NASB) says it this way: "This I say therefore, and affirm together with the Lord, that you walk no longer just as the Gentiles walk, in the **futility of their mind, being darkened in their understanding, EXCLUDED FROM THE LIFE OF GOD**, because of the ignorance that is in them, because of the **hardness of their heart.**" Now look at verses 20-21 and write them here.

The real question is this: "Is your life about you, or about what God wants to do in you and through you?"

Hearing the word of God produces faith in the hearer.

Notice, in verse 21 it speaks of **hearing** about Jesus. Every day, there will be the voice of the Lord, and the voice of the world. Whatever we subject our minds to will determine which becomes more real to us. Look back at Romans 10:17. What does hearing the Word produce? _____. Now look at Ephesians 4:18. What will be the result if we walk in the futility of our mind by listening to the world?

_____ and _____

_____ What does it say will happen to our heart? _____

_____

When you hear the phrase, "excluded from the life of God", what does that mean for you?

UNBELIEF IS DEADLY!!! The fear of the Lord comes into play here. Look up Proverbs 1:7 and write it here.

A simple definition of the fear of the Lord is simply that God means what He says. Faith knows that God means every good thing – every promise – that He gives. It also knows that God means every warning. He is deadly serious. Check out James 4:4. Paraphrase it here.

How does that relate with Ephesians 4: 17-18 we looked at earlier?

I need to repeat: **UNBELIEF IS DEADLY**…God has amazing plans for us. When we saturate our minds with truth, we will walk in truth and freedom; when we saturate our minds with the world's lies (futility of our mind), we will be separated from the life God desires for us. The choice always lies in our court.

Let's take one more side trip. A wise person can avoid much grief by taking the opportunity to learn through observation. Let's look at the Israelites as they considered entering the promise land, and see what we can learn from their example. Read Exodus 23: 20-30. Who were all the people God said were going to be in the promise

land (verse 23) _____

_____.

What did God say He was going to do to them? (paraphrase verses 27-28)

Week 4 - Freedom From Unbelief

Now turn to Numbers 13: 1-2, 21-29. Who did they find in the land? (verse 29)

_____

Do you see God had already told them those enemies were going to be there, but

that He would drive them out before them? _____ Continuing in Numbers 13:

30-33, what were the two reports given? _____

and _____ Look at Numbers 14:1-4

to see the people's response. _____.

One report agreed with what God had already told them. The other report was based on their human eyes and understanding (the futility of their mind). Approximately 1500 years later, in the book of Hebrews, God is still speaking of how frustrated He was with these people. Read Hebrews 3: 8-11. In verses 8 and 10, His disappointment is not in their actions, but in the condition of their hearts. Write verse 12

Unbelief in God's word causes our hearts to become hardened.

What does verse 13 say causes a hardened heart? _____

The Israelites chose the report based on circumstances in front of them, and forgot

the faithfulness God had shown throughout their journey. In verse 15, when does He

ask us not to harden our hearts? _____

Notice the word, "hear", once again. Faith comes by hearing God's word. When we hear it, we have a choice of hardening our hearts, or turning in faith, trusting Him, and obeying.

Unbelief in God's word causes our hearts to become hardened. God calls that sin. It needs to be confessed as such. In last week's lesson, we went through the steps we need to take when God points out sin in our lives. We will look deeper into this issue called FAITH tomorrow, but for now, take time to ask the Lord if there are areas you have trusted the ideas and voice of the world, over the voice of God. Take time to go through the necessary steps of forgiveness and freedom. We'll take another trip tomorrow… we'll walk through some more pages of God's Word. It's full of amazing stories, but more importantly, it is full of Truth that sets us free. Take time to talk to the author of the book…See you tomorrow…

WEEK 4 - FREEDOM FROM UNBELIEF

Faith is sometimes an obscure word…by that, I mean faith is one of those things hard to explain, and even sometimes to understand. Let's do some searching through scripture to see if we can get a handle on what faith looks like in our individual lives. This lesson requires more reading than normal, but it also gives an opportunity to instill valuable insights concerning our "father of faith"…and even more valuable insights about our own journey. We'll begin with Romans 5:1. What does faith do for

us? _____

We see here, that faith has power in the supernatural/spiritual realm. Look further down to verse 4. When God takes us through hard times, what one word describes

the end result He is after at the end of this verse? _____ Verse 5 says

that **HOPE** does not disappoint … For that to be true…for HOPE to not disappoint, there has to be a substance for that hope. It cannot be simply wishful thinking. Turn with me to Romans 15: 4 (NASB) and fill in the blanks. "For whatever was written in earlier times was written for our instruction, that through perseverance and the

_____ we might have _____." Verse 13

says God wants us to _____ in hope. That's not just a little sprin-

kling…God wants us to overflow!!! So let's go in search of hope…we just might find where it comes from

Turn to Hebrews 11:1 Let's begin with the good ole King James version. Write it here, then write your version after it..

For HOPE to not disappoint, there has to be a substance for that hope.

Without faith, hope is just a whimsical feeling.

King James actually calls faith a substance, which would mean it would be something we can grab hold of. Other versions call it assurance or confidence. That still implies an embraceable force. Without faith, hope is just a whimsical feeling. There is no anchor to stabilize the object…nothing to keep the wind from swaying it to and fro, taking it off track. HOWEVER, many people claim to have faith…the world likes to tell us it doesn't matter WHAT you believe, as long as you believe. **OH, SO WRONG!!!** Looking

back to Romans 15:4, if we are going to have true hope, where must it come from?

_____ As we return to He-

brews 11 and begin perusing the verses that follow, we see by faith we understand that the seen is created from the unseen (verse 3)…that God is looking for a submitted heart (verse 4)…that we will obey when we don't know why God has asked (verse 7), or where He is taking us (verse 8)…that our anchor is in Him alone (verse 10).

We are also given insight from the Holy Spirit. Hebrews 11:6 is a familiar verse. Let's take a closer look. Write it here:

How many times have we forfeited peace, deliverance, healing, and provision, because we have forgotten God exists?

The NIV links the first thought in that verse with the last two, by using the word BE-

CAUSE. It says to please God we must believe He _____ AND that _____

_____. God loves it when

you come to Him - BECAUSE you don't talk to someone you don't believe exists. However, there is that second part that delights His heart. He waits with anticipation…just waiting for us to come and allow Him to move on our behalf. How many times have we forfeited peace, deliverance, healing, and provision, because we have forgotten God exists? Maybe we know He exists in the heavens, but sometimes forget He exists as our Abba Father…and we are His child.

Sounds like it's time for another story. Let's look at someone like us. God actually calls him a man of faith. Some of the things we will learn should encourage us in our own walk…isn't that what Romans 15:4 says?

We'll start with the background for the story. I'm sure you know the story of Abraham, but all stories need a backdrop. To do this, we need to travel all the way back to the 11th chapter of Genesis. In verse 29 we first find Abram and his wife, Sarai. They traveled with Abram's father towards the land of Canaan, but settled in Haran along the way. There, Abram's father died. Chapter 12 is where the Lord appears to Abram with a directive coupled with a promise. Verses 2-4 tell us what would happen if Abram would leave this land and go where God would show him. Paraphrase verses 2-4:

Notice Abram is 75 years old at this point. Now look at verse 7, and write the first sentence of that verse.

If God is promising to give this land to Abram's descendents, what does this say about the possibility of Abram and Sarai having at least one child?

_____ Unfortunately, we don't have to go far to see this

"man of faith" start to tarnish his halo….look at verses 10-20. If Abram truly believed God was going to fulfill His promise, wouldn't he know that no one was going to kill

him simply because he had a beautiful wife? _____ Evidently, Abram didn't

truly KNOW God at this point. If we were to go directly from this point to Romans 4, we would simply shake our heads. That portion of scripture speaks of the amazing Abraham who chose to believe God's promise, in spite of all circumstances coming against him…doesn't look like the same guy. That's what happens when we are on a journey…sometimes, the beginning doesn't in any way resemble the end. Amazingly, even in Abram's failure to trust God, the Lord blesses him on his journey. Be careful when judging someone who's on a journey…even when that someone is you. (Sometimes it's easier to extend grace to another person's tarnished halo, than to extend that same grace to ourselves. Just saying…)

Be careful when judging someone who's on a journey…even when that someone is you.

Chapter 2 of Abram's story…Abram and his nephew Lot have both become wealthy with much livestock…so much that the area will no longer support both of them. Abram graciously allows Lot to select his area, and then settles in to the area that is left. Let's look at Genesis 13: 14-17. Who does God promise to give the land?

_____ _____. How many descendants does God

promise to give him? _____.

Many things take place after that, and several years pass. God visits Abram once more

in Chapter 15. The entire chapter makes excellent reading, but for now we will concentrate on the first 5 verses. In verse 2, Abram questions God about who his heir will be. It

appears it will simply be a servant in his home. What is God's response to that in verse

4? _____ What about

in verse 5?_____

Verse 6 is the beginning of Abram's true walk of faith. Record it here:

WEEK 4 - FREEDOM FROM UNBELIEF

Even though we will see more struggles, this one statement has become the basis for salvation. It is quoted three times in the New Testament, where we are even called heirs of the promise if our walk coincides with his. God comes into covenant at this point in Abram's life, and foretells of the Egyptian captivity and deliverance of his descendants.

Chapter 16 is about another tarnished halo…Ishmael. You know the story. Abram is now 85 years old…no son. Sarai has an idea that almost trumps Eve's. Why not take matters into our own hands…let me give you Hagar, my maid, and you can have a child through her? **REALLY BAD IDEA**…and Abram agreed **(another bad idea)** At 86 years of age, Abram became the father of a son…not the promised one, but a son. History has shown what that one choice has caused. Adam's sin brought sin into the world…Abram's sin brought conflict and destruction to the same world. The Lord told Abram that Ishmael's descendants would be against everyone, and everyone would be against them. We see both sins played out in the world today.

Adam's sin brought sin into the world… Abram's sin brought conflict and destruction to the same world.

The Lord appears once more to Abram, this time when he is 99 years old. Look at

Genesis 17: 5. God changed Abram's name to _____.

He then said he would be the father of _____

The journey of faith isn't something we are born into… it is a walk.

Catch the fact that now he would be the father of a multitude of NATIONS…not just descendants. We, the Gentiles, are now included as children of Abraham. An interesting side note is that Abraham was then circumcised. When he fathered Ishmael, it was before he was in covenant with God. Isaac is the son of the covenant. BUT POOR ABRAHAM'S HALO is about to be tarnished again. Chapter 20 tells the sad tale. Abraham now relocates and, once again, fears the King will kill him because of Sarah's beauty. (Sarah is now 89 years old…wow, to be that beautiful at 89!). The king takes her into his harem, but he has a dream, where the Lord tells him Sarah is Abraham's wife. He is furious with Abraham and releases her. Do you see what the enemy was trying to do here? If Sarah had slept with Abimelech, there would have been no proof that Isaac was truly God's gift to Abraham. God was determined to set the record straight.

We just walked through the circumstances and saw the crooked path, yet God declares Abraham full of faith.

This story is getting long, but I want to give you a clear picture of the journey of faith. It isn't something we are born into…it is a walk. By the time Genesis 21 comes into play, Sarah, at the age of 90, and Abraham, at the age of 100, hold the promise of God in their arms. It has taken them 25 years. This takes us to Romans 4:18-22. It is a glorious tale of Abraham's faith. We just walked through the circumstances and saw the crooked path, yet God declares Abraham full of faith. Let's look at the lessons God says Abraham learned along the way. Record the first sentence of verse 18 from the NLT.

Week 4 - Freedom From Unbelief

Look at what it says in verse 19 in your version. What we need to see here, is that Abraham did not ignore the facts. He looked them straight in the eye. In his story, one thing Abraham never did was question whether God COULD DO what He said He WOULD DO. Write verses 20-21 here:

This is what was reckoned to Abraham as righteousness…not his perfect actions but his heart for God. That should give us hope as we continue on our journey. It doesn't give us an excuse to sin…we know that…but it gives us hope that we, too, may be called a friend of God, even when our journey seems to take several curves…and we find ourselves wearing a tarnished halo.

This is what was reckoned to Abraham as righteousness…not his perfect actions but his heart for God.

We saw in Hebrews 3: 9-19 that faith is a heart issue. It is also a choice. It doesn't depend on your circumstances. It doesn't depend on your feelings. I'm sure Abraham wasn't feeling very faithful as he looked at his body and that of Sarah's, but it says, "with respect to the promise of God, he did not waiver in unbelief, but grew strong in faith, giving glory to God." That would mean he had to fight through everything that would come against God's word. It also means that the battle usually starts and ends with the mind. When our mind accepts circumstances as truth, then circumstances rule. When we use God's word as our measuring stick, then God's word rules. Let's end today's study by instilling one more truth into our being. What does 2 Corinthians 10:5 say we are to do concerning every thought that comes our way?

What we allow our mind to think will determine what we believe…and that will determine the person we become.

The battle is first fought in our mind. Our eyes see, our ears hear, our nose smells, our mouth tastes, and our feelings feel…but what we allow our mind to think will determine what we believe…and that will determine the person we become.

Faith – it's what we believe. The choice is ours.

You will notice there are only two days in our workbook this week. Spend the remainder of your days reviewing what you have learned thus far concerning God's Word, Forgiveness, Unconfessed Sin, and Unbelief. We want to make sure we're not just skimming the surface. God wants to do a mighty work within each one of us. Let's partner with Him to accomplish that. That's what faith is all about!!!

FREEDOM Through Obedience

You can obey God and still have a disobedient spirit – if you obey Him only because you agree with Him, and won't obey if you don't agree.

Luke 10: 27 You shall love the Lord your God with all your _____,

and with all your _____ and with all your _____

and with all your _____

Leviticus. 20:6-8 God will set His face _____ anyone who trusts in

mediums or those who consult the spirits of the dead.

GOD'S DIVINE GOVERNMENT

Gen. 1:1 In the beginning _____ created the heavens and the earth.

Genesis 1: 26 God _____ man and gave them _____

over everything on the earth.

We are the _____ ones and God is the

_____.

HIS WORD COMMANDS THAT WE SUBMIT TO HIM

James 4:6 God _____ the proud but gives _____

to the humble.

I Peter 5:8 _____ and _____ allows God

to fight for us.

WEEK FIVE - FREEDOM THROUGH OBEDIENCE

WHAT GOD'S WORD SAYS ABOUT LISTENING AND OBEYING HIM

Proverbs 15:31-33 Before _____ comes

_____.

Proverbs 2:6-8 The Lord gives _____.

Proverbs 3:1-18 Obedience is a _____ issue.

Proverbs 16:25 There is a way that seems _____, but it ends in

_____

Proverbs 19:27 If you stop listening to instruction, you will _____

from the words of knowledge.

Psalm. 107, 10,11 Rebellion against God's Word is seeing what He says about

something and choosing to call Him a _____ and believe what you

_____ to believe.

I Samuel 15:22-24 God doesn't take _____ or

_____ lightly.

Deuteronomy 8:16 Any of God's testing or humbling is to do us _____ in

the end.

Psalm. 51: 10-13 Ask God to reveal any stubbornness or rebellion in your life. Seek His forgiveness for anything He shows you. Then ask Him to sustain you with a willing spirit.

NOTES:

WEEK FIVE - FREEDOM THROUGH OBEDIENCE

Today is a transition day. We will be transitioning between unbelief and disobedience. These two issues may not seem to be related, but they are actually intertwined. If we don't really believe what God says is true, then why obey? It's not going to matter one way or the other. We need God's Word on the subject…so let's begin in a now familiar passage, Hebrews 3:16-19, especially 18-19. Here come those Israelites again! Definitely don't want to be like them, but if we don't learn from their mistakes, we could easily fall into the same trap. Verse 18 both asks a question, and gives the answer. The

question is, "Who did God swear would not enter His rest?". Write the answer. _____

_____ Continue down to verse 19. Why does

it say they won't be able to enter? _____ Do you see the

correlation here between disobedience and unbelief? God says they were disobedient, then goes on to say it was because of unbelief. When we truly believe in our heart that what God is saying is true, we will obey what He says.

It might be good to check out another story. This one is located in 1 Samuel 15. The first three verses set the stage for this event. Samuel delivered God's edict to King Saul. The Lord was going to punish ungodly Amalek for what he did to Israel. Paraphrase what he tells Saul he is to do to Amalek, found in verse 3.

So we know what he was supposed to do. Let's see if he obeyed. Read verses 7-9. Did

he defeat the Amalekites? _____ Did he obey the words "utterly destroy all that he

has, and do not spare him; but put to death both man and woman, child and infant,

ox and sheep, camel and donkey."? _____ Look at verses 19-21. Saul was apparently ignorant that he sinned. If he had truly believed strict obedience was necessary,

would he have spared the king and animals? _____

Saul and the Israelites both fell into the same sin. What was that sin? _____

God says they were disobedient, then goes on to say it was because of unbelief.

Verse 11 shows us God's response to disobedience. 1 Samuel 15: 22-23 hold the

well known words from Samuel. Let's look at them and fill in the blanks. (NASB) "And Samuel said, "Has the Lord as much delight in burnt offerings and sacrifices as in

_____ the voice of the Lord? Behold, to _____ is _____

than _____, and to _____ (give careful attention to) than the fat

of rams. For _____ is as the sin of _____ (witch-

craft), and _____ (stubbornness) is as _____ and

_____. Because you have _____ the

_____ of the Lord, He has also _____ you from being

king.

Saul thought he could take what God said to do and change it however he thought best. God called that rebellion

Let's dissect this passage. How did Saul justify his actions in verses 20-21? _____

_____. Turn to Isaiah 55: 8-9. Write them here:

Saul thought he could take what God said to do and change it however he thought best. God called that rebellion, which would be the highest form of disobedience. We need to rethink this…what is it saying to us…and possibly about us? 1 Samuel 15:19 is a question Samuel asks Saul. Write the first sentence here.

Can you think of times you have known God asked you to do something, yet you determined how fully you needed to obey, and how much you could explain away? When Samuel confronts Saul concerning his sin, what reason does Saul give for sin-

ning? (verse 24). _____. Remember

from our previous studies, we have a choice whether we listen to the world, or listen to the voice of God. Here is an example of a king who disobeyed God, because he honored people above God.

WEEK FIVE - FREEDOM THROUGH OBEDIENCE

Even after he admitted his sin, look at verse 30. Right after he admits his sin, what does

he ask Samuel to do? _____

What is he more concerned about – his sin or his honor before the people? _____

_____. The fear of man is deadly.

Look up Proverbs 29:25. Write it here:

Saul fell into that snare. When he went out to battle, he probably had no intention of disobeying God's command to him. However, when the frenzy of battle took over, and people began shouting out their ideas, Saul got caught up in his desire to please the people, instead of choosing the fear of the Lord. The fear of man can drive us to do things we never dreamed we would do.

How can we protect ourselves from falling into that trap? Look up James 1:21 _____

_____

_____

_____ The first thing it tells us to do, is to get rid of

The fear of man can drive us to do things we never dreamed we would do.

all filthiness and wickedness. That sounds like repentance…back to confessing those sins! The question might arise: "Won't I ever be finished with this repentance stuff?"… the answer to that is a resounding NO! Philippians 1:6 tells us that God is going to be working on us until Jesus returns. Our response simply needs to be to continue letting Him do what He earnestly desires to do…conforming us into the image of His Son.

After telling us to get rid of all of that junk, God then invites us to humbly accept His word that He desires to plant deep within our hearts, thereby saving our souls. Now, that's an interesting phrase…saving our souls. What could that possibly mean? Aren't we saved the moment we accept Jesus as our Lord and Savior? The answer to that last question is a resounding "YES"! The moment we do that, we are born again and experience salvation. How, then, does that differ from saving our souls? To answer that, we need a few definitions.

We are created as a three part being – body, spirit and soul. Our body is simply that physical frame used to hold the real us. Our spirit is that eternal part of us that communes with God. (1 Corinthians 2:10-16). It is the part that is reborn when we accept Christ (John 3:6). Our soul is our mind, will, and emotions. It is the part that gets trained by either the word of God or the world, circumstances and the devil. From the very beginning, our mind is being told what to think, our emotions are being told what to feel, and our will is being taught what we should choose. Unless we are careful to take every thought captive, we become a product of our environment.

James 3:13-18 explains the different types of wisdom. "Wisdom" that would teach us to walk in bitter jealousy and selfish ambition is described in verse 15. Write that verse here.

What have you been doing lately to immerse yourself in God's word?

Verse 16 tells us what results in this kind of wisdom. _____

Take time to describe God's wisdom according to verse 17.

Verse 18 speaks of sowing in peace…aaahh…that sounds sweet to the soul. Finally, the last part of James 1:21 says that as we allow God's word to become planted deep within our souls, it actually brings salvation and freedom to that area of our lives. Write out 2 Timothy 3:16-17.

It teaches, reproves, corrects, and trains in righteousness. It is mandatory for our spiritual growth. What have you been doing lately to immerse yourself in God's word?

God doesn't require daily reading of His word simply because He wants to give us some compulsory job description. As with all of God's ways, He has a reason. Psalm 19:7-11 is a beautiful portion of scripture that speaks of how God created His word to work in our lives. Verse 7 even begins by speaking of the advantages to our soul. Write that portion here.

The rest of those verses makes good reading. Let's slip down to verse 11, and write it here also.

Saul would have done good to listen to God's word when He spoke to him through Samuel. We are fortunate today to have His written word that is so available to us. We might want to excuse Saul by saying he didn't realize the importance of following the word totally. Even if we would do that for him, verse 11 tells us that we are without excuse. We have the word…we have the warnings…we have the promises. "In keeping them there is great reward." Happy reading…the promises are waiting…

We have the word…we have the warnings…we have the promises. "In keeping them there is great reward."

WEEK FIVE - FREEDOM THROUGH OBEDIENCE

O h, the joy of obedience! God's Word says in Hebrews 3:11 and 4:3, that He had a rest just waiting for the children of Israel, if they would simply obey what He was asking them to do. Hebrews 3: 18-19 tells us they missed it because of unbelief and disobedience. The question we need to ask is, "what happened to that rest?" Did it go away when the children of Israel failed to embrace it? Was it just for them?

Let's look at Hebrews 4:1.

Rest would be freedom from needing to be justified by our works.

Underline what it says about the present availability of the promise. Look at verse

2. Why was the message they heard of no value to them? _____

_____ Check out verse 3. Whose rest is God speaking of?

_____ Look now at verses 4 and 10 (NIV) and fill in the blanks. (Verse 4)

"On the seventh day God _____ from His _____," (Verse 10)

for those who _____ God's _____ also _____

from their _____, just as _____ did from His. What do you

think of when you contemplate resting from your "works"? _____

_____

Ephesians 2: 8-9 says we are saved through faith (the opposite of unbelief). It is not something we do; it is a gift from God. Write verse 9

The word "works" comes up again. Works in this verse might be defined as a group of commandments that must be perfectly kept in order to qualify for salvation. Check out Galatians 2:16 (NASB) and fill in the blanks. "Nevertheless, knowing

that a man is not _____ by the _____ of the Law but

through _____ in Christ Jesus, even we have believed in Christ Jesus,

that we may be _____ by _____ in Christ, and _____

by _____ of the Law; since by the _____ of the Law shall no

flesh be _____." REST would be freedom from needing to be justified by

our works. WHAT PEACE!!! I'm sure you and I both agree that is the life we want to choose.

Look back at Hebrews 4:1. There is a warning for us to not be like the Israelites, who failed to enter that rest. We'd better do some more reading…

Look at Hebrews 4: 6 and 11. What one word kept them out of the promise land

(where they would enter into the rest God had for them)? _____.

Something interesting is to notice the following verse 12. Write it here:

God desires to reveal the root issues – He's not interested in merely dealing with symptoms. He loves us way too much for that.

God's Word does amazing things; however, for this lesson let's look at the very last

thing in that verse that the Word does. _____

_____ _____ Read verse 13. I think the NIV says it

best. Do you see that God's Word is the one thing that will uncover anything within our heart that would keep us from obeying? As we continue in our study, we will discover over and over that God desires to reveal the root issues – He's not interested in merely dealing with symptoms. He loves us way too much for that.

True obedience is tested when God's ways and our ways collide.

Obedience is pretty easy…as long as life is good, and God is doing things OUR way, it's pretty easy to obey. The problem is, that's not really obedience – it's just doing what we agree with. True obedience is tested when God's ways and our ways collide. That's what really shows our heart. Remembering Isaiah 55:7-9, we realize God's thoughts and our thoughts don't tend to be the same…and God isn't changing His mind… that's because His thoughts and ways are higher than ours. If we walk in wisdom, we don't want Him to change His mind; instead, we want Him to change OUR thoughts and mind. Of course, HIS way of doing that is crosswise to what we would choose. We're going to look at some more scripture references concerning this. We will use Jesus as our example…look at Hebrews 5: 7-9. Interestingly, Jesus learned obedience by

_____ How could that be?!!? Look at

Hebrews 2: 10. How did God choose to perfect Jesus? _____

_____.

90

WEEK FIVE - FREEDOM THROUGH OBEDIENCE

Do you see that, if Jesus didn't have to choose to obey God, even though He was suffering, then His "perfection" wouldn't have been complete? As I said earlier, obedience is easy as long as life is easy. How could God ask us to obey Him in the hard issues of life, if His Son wasn't asked to do the same? With Jesus as our example, we see that we, also, are perfected through the things we suffer. 2 Chronicles 16:9 is a good reference. Let's look at it – it's worth writing down:

How does He know our hearts are completely His, if we are not ever asked to obey in the hard times? The children of Israel faced giants. Sometimes, it's easy for us to find fault with them, but place yourself in their shoes. What would you have honestly done, if you were the one facing the prospect of fighting those giants? Yet, God was looking for hearts through which He could show Himself strong. He didn't find it in them…so now He offers us the same chance to enter into the rest… to enter into all He desires to give us…to show Himself strong on our behalf. He isn't asking something of us He never asked of anyone else…He tests us in the same way He tested His Son…think about it. God is after a heart that is completely His, so that He can show Himself strong on their behalf…What an opportunity!

How could God ask us to obey Him in the hard issues of life, if His Son wasn't asked to do the same?

God is after a heart that is completely His, so that He can show Himself strong on their behalf… What an opportunity!

One last scripture reference to consider today. I love Psalm 81 – it would be well worth reading the entire Psalm. For our lesson today, we will focus on verses 13, 14, 16 (NASB). (13) Oh that my people would _____ to me, that Israel would _____.

(14) I would quickly _____ their _____, and turn my hand _____ their _____. (16) I would feed you with the _____ of _____, and with _____ from the _____ I would _____ _____.

What is the requirement given in verse 13, that will produce the benefits in verses 14 & 16? _____ A one word answer to that could be obedience. Circle what God says He will do for you if you obey. There are definitely benefits to obedience. Tomorrow we will look at the ramifications of disobedience, but for today, enjoy that blissful rest God longs to give you…of course, in order to do that, you will need to practice obedience…happy practicing…

Week Five - Freedom Through Obedience

I love happy endings. Most movies I watch are because I know that's how they will end. I don't like movies that end in sorrow or heartache…I avoid watching those whenever

I can. God likes happy endings, too. The last part of 2Peter 3: 9 shows us God's heart.

It says He is patient towards us _____

_____. That's how He wants all of our lives to end…with

a happy hug as He welcomes us into His Kingdom. Deuteronomy 10: 12-13 confirms this. Paraphrase what God asks us to do:

God not only wants a happy ending for us, He tells us how we can cooperate with Him to make sure it happens

The last part of verse 13 tells us why He asks us to do that. Write it here. _____

_____. You see, God not only wants a happy ending for us, He tells us how

we can cooperate with Him to make sure it happens…and it is definitely for our good to do so!

Yesterday, we talked about that beautiful rest God has designed for us…but there is another side of the story that must be told. It is the part that gives us a choice… remember, God always gives us a choice because, without a choice, there is no opportunity for true relationship. We're going to be delving into Proverbs on today's journey. The first six verses of Proverbs 1 promise us great wisdom, understanding, discernment and instruction. That sounds like a good place to go if we are wanting to know God's thoughts and ways. Write Proverbs 1:7 here:

The fear of the Lord is simply knowing God means what He says…all His promises are true… and so are His warnings.

Earlier we learned that the fear of the Lord is simply knowing God means what He says…all His promises are true…and so are His warnings. The portion of scripture we are going to study is rather lengthy, but well worth the time. Let's begin in Proverbs 1:23.

Circle what God promises to do if we listen when He corrects us. Good stuff!!! We would love to end our story right here, and everyone applaud…but wait…there's more. Look at

verses 24-25. What type of person is He referring to here? _____.

Would you agree that they could be called disobedient? _____ Can you re-member some childhood incidents where you were disobedient, and then were

found out? _____ Was what happened next a pleasant or painful experience?

_____

A costly story…There was a time in my younger years as a Christian where I clear-ly heard God's direction, but chose to lean on my own understanding. The con-sequence was a bible study that split apart, and God wasn't able to accomplish all He had planned. I was actually teaching these very lessons. The subject of healing came up in the class, and I knew the answers! I knew God's will is for healing today – and it is…I knew God wants us to pray for healing and expect Him to answer – and He does. In spite of the strong check in my spirit…in spite of hearing clearly from God in the depths of my heart…I chose to lean on my own understanding, and speak of my conviction, even quoting scriptures. There is a right time and a right place to speak. God was clearly telling me this was neither. Our own understanding can never tell us the history of those to whom we are speaking. It was a painfully hot topic with two of the women attending. It was not only something they could not accept, it changed their ability to listen and receive any of the teachings that God could have used in so many areas of their lives. God knew that – I didn't. The consequences were painful both to them, and to me. It took years to rebuild those relationships, and I'm not sure that has been fully done to this day. Consequences can be painful and costly.

Returning to Proverbs 1, what are the consequences God says will happen in verse

26, if we refuse to listen to Him over and over? _____

_____ Verse 27 says that dread,

calamity, distress and anguish await us…not a very good ending for anyone's story… but that's not the worst part of it all. Look at verse 28. We would like to think that, no matter how many times we spurn God's counsel and spit in His face, He will always hear and rescue us when we call out to Him. Verses 29 and 30 show us the reason He has turned His back. It would be good to write them here. Sometimes writing things down helps us remember.

Week Five - Freedom Through Obedience

What do those verses say about their fear of the Lord? _____

_____ Does that help you begin to understand how

important that is? _____ Again, look at verses 31 & 32. What does verse 32 say

the end result will be? _____.

HOWEVER....YES!!! HOWEVER... God is all about giving choices, and He, too, loves a happy ending. Notice how He began in verse 23…promises of good things when we listen to Him. Look at how He ends this section in verse 33. Write what His promise is for those who listen and obey.

_____

Obedience plays a fundamental part of choosing life

It would be good for us to refresh ourselves with the passage in Deuteronomy 30: 19-

20. Who is God calling to witness our choice? _____

What are our choices? _____ or _____; the _____

or the _____

Who chooses? _____ Who does it affect? _____.

What three things does verse 20 say are necessary steps to choose life?

Notice how obedience plays a fundamental part of choosing life.

Let's look at one last section today: Isaiah 48: 17-19. What are the two things verse 17

says God wants to do? _____ and _____

_____. What does verse 18 say would be necessary for that

to happen? _____ What is the result

if we do that? _____ and _____

_____. Finally, look at verse 19. What

does the first part say about our descendants? _____

_____

What amazing promise does He give at the end of that verse?

Obedience…
oh, how sweet the
sound…oh, how
sweet the reward.

Obedience…oh, how sweet the sound…oh, how sweet the reward. May the thought of that happy "Jesus hug" draw you into sweet, obedient fellowship with your Creator.

Another week with the opportunity to take the next few days to study and pray over what you are learning. Don't pass up these opportunities and simply see them as free days to focus on other things. God wants to embed His word and His ways within our heart. Allow Him to reveal new truths to you personally... truths that will truly set you free!!!

FREEDOM OF THE TONGUE

Proverbs 18:20-21 _____ and _____ are in the power of the tongue.

Deuteronomy 30:19, 20 God has set before us _____ and

_____

THE CHOICE IS _____.

Matthew 12:37 By our _____ we will be justified.

By our _____ we will be condemned.

Matthew 12:34 The mouth speaks from what fills the _____.

Psalm 33:6-9 The world was created by the _____ of God.

DO WE HAVE CREATIVE POWER WITH OUR TONGUE?

Mark 11:23-25 We have authority to _____ to the mountains in our lives.

Psalm 141:3 To set a guard over my mouth, I must deal with the issues in my

_____

Proverbs 4:23 Watch over your _____ with all diligence for from it flow the issues of life.

Week Six - Freedom of the Tongue

WHAT IS GOD'S WILL FOR US?

Ephesians 4:15-25 Speak the _____ in _____.

Ephesians 4:29-30 Let go of _____ unwholesome words.

Col 4:6 Let your speech be _____ and seasoned with

_____.

Job 22:27-28 AFTER LAYING YOUR GOLD IN THE DUST AND PICKING UP GOD

AS YOUR GOLD: 1). You will pray to God; **2).** He will hear you; **3). THEN** you shall

_____ a thing and it shall be _____ for you.

Isaiah 54:17 IT IS _____ RESPONSIBILITY TO _____ EVERY

TONGUE THAT RISES UP TO ACCUSE YOU IN JUDGMENT.

It is also _____ responsibility to take ownership of any sin or sinful at-

titude that needs _____ , _____, and then receiving

_____.

**Ask God to fill your heart with the knowledge of His Word & a revelation that
His Word is true.**

NOTES:

Week Six - Freedom of the Tongue

Oh, that tongue!!! James 3:2 tells us, if we can control our tongue, we can control everything about us. The question then arises: "What is it about the tongue that has so much power and significance?" Good question that deserves an honest answer. So, let's get started on this leg of our study. Remember, we are still headed True North on this journey…which means God's Word, as our roadmap, is still in place.

In our first week's lesson we learned that the sum of God's Word is truth. Many times, if we combine several scriptures of the same topic, we get a much deeper, clearer picture of what God is telling us. Let's begin with two such scriptures. The first is, by now, a very familiar verse – Deuteronomy 30: 19. Read it and fill in

the blanks (NASB) I call _____ and _____ to witness

against you today that I have set before you _____ and _____,

the _____ and the _____. So choose

_____ that you may _____, you and your

_____. What are the first two things God says He sets

before us? _____ and _____. Keep that in mind, and

now look at Proverbs 18:21. _____ and _____ are in the

power of the _____, and those who _____ will

_____ its _____. What is in the power of the tongue?

_____ and _____. What choice did God give

us in Deuteronomy 30:19? _____ and _____. Do you see

God's ultimate desire is for our heart to be completely His.

that when we speak, we are creating either life or death, and the choice is ours? I'm not taking us back and forth through those scriptures so we can see a riddle…I am taking us through the maize so we can see the strong connection between the use of our tongue, and the choice of life or death.

I have a salad bowl full of truths about our words, hearts, thoughts and how all of them combine together to impact our lives and the world we live in. I have tried unsuccessfully to separate the issues, but it is like trying to separate the items in a salad bowl once they are mixed. You can be somewhat successful dividing out the larger items, but it is really the combination, and the dressing, that makes the taste complete. Therefore, I am going to present a "salad bowl" of thoughts for this week's study. Our aim will be to discover the correlation between our words, thoughts, and heart. One basic truth…perhaps the most important one…is that God's ultimate desire is for our heart to be completely His. Remember 2 Chronicles 16:9. Just for fun, look it up and write the first part of it here – it's a good one to memorize.

WEEK SIX - FREEDOM OF THE TONGUE

Words – Heart – Thoughts –Those would be the larger items in this salad bowl. Let's start with Words…what's so important about the words we speak?…Hmmm…Let's find the answer in the most reliable place possible…God's Word. Start by writing out Matthew 12:36-37

Our words reveal the truth of what is in our heart.

In verse 36, what will be the basis for our judgment? _____

Our words will do one of two things. What are those two things? _____

_____ Those are pretty strong words…but who said

them? _____ We find the reason for this statement in the last part of verse 34.

Write that part here.

If it came out of your mouth, it came directly from your heart.

There is that heart connection again…our words reveal the truth of what is in our heart. It would do us well to listen to the words that come out of our mouths. In fact, I challenge you to do that this week. Make a mental note…better yet, keep a list of those words that have surprised you, when you think of them in this context.

A couple of thoughts…don't fall into the trap of saying, "Oh, I didn't mean that." If it came out of your mouth, it came directly from your heart. Also, don't give yourself the excuse of, "Oh, I am just tired." Or, "I just don't feel good." Those are times your guard is down, and things slip out of your mouth (from your heart) that you would have kept hidden, because they aren't socially acceptable. As you recognize those "no-no words", you might make a note of them here.

This will give you a window into your heart…

Speaking of our heart…let's look at God's desire for our heart. Deuteronomy 5: 29 is a good place to start. Record it here.

What are the two things God wants our heart to do? _____

and _____ What is His promise if

we do those things? _____

_____ Who does that affect? _____ Remember, we

He doesn't just want our obedience…He wants obedience from a heart that is totally His.

learned in our study of obedience, that God said He would feed us with the finest of wheat, if we would simply obey Him when He speaks. However, He doesn't just want our obedience…He wants obedience from a heart that is totally His. One more scripture – Luke 12:34 Write it here.

God wants to be your treasure…your most prized possession. In Genesis 15:1, God tells Abraham that He is his very great reward. He wants our hearts to see Him as that. Through these scriptures today, the Lord is saying to us that His desire is towards us, and He longs for our desire to be towards Him.

What is your treasure? What do you think about… long for…dream of? We need to be careful, because our treasure can begin to define us. Look up Proverbs 23:7 (KJV) and write the first sentence here.

That tells us that what we choose to think will eventually become who we are. Heavy stuff…but oh, so necessary to know.

LET ME SUMMARIZE FOR TODAY.

• Whatever a person chooses to give their thoughts to, will eventually affect their heart. (As a man thinks in his heart so he is.)

• What I allow to reside in my heart will come out of my mouth. (Out of the abundance of the heart the mouth speaks.)

• I can discover what is in my heart by listening to the words coming from my mouth…

• **THAT REVELATION IS THE FIRST STEP NECESSARY FOR CHANGE.**

Instead of salad tomorrow, I think I'll try a smorgasbord. Until then, listen to what you speak…it just may surprise you.

Whatever *a person chooses to give their thoughts to, will eventually affect their heart.*

WEEK SIX - FREEDOM OF THE TONGUE

A smorgasbord and a salad bowl have a lot of the same characteristics, and yet definitely have their own personalities. Both have a variety of ingredients; however, the items in a salad tend to lose their individual identity; whereas, the items on a smorgasbord are definitely distinct. I took the ingredients, "Words – Heart – Thoughts", from the salad bowl yesterday and blended them together. Today, I am going to select those same ingredients from our smorgasbord and look at them as distinct, yet connected, items.

It is our thoughts that actually begin the process, so that's where we will begin today. If it is true that our thoughts have the power to define us, it would behoove us to start by determining who we want to be. In that way, we will have a grasp on the kind of thoughts we need to entertain.

If we truly want to change, we need to begin with our thought processing.

What better place to begin than 1 Corinthians 13: 4-7. It would be good for us to write the verses.

Let's look closely at these verses. Circle the words that portray love. Does that describe someone you would like to be? More importantly, does that describe who you are today? There are probably areas where each of us would admit we need to improve. The question then would be, "How do I do that?" Proverbs 23:7 told us that we become what we think, therefore if we truly want to change, we need to begin with our thought processing. Romans 12:2 will show us our first step. Write it out so you can look at it closely.

What are we told NOT to do? _____ If we look at the

world's definition of "love" today, we discover a slippery slope. True love does not enable others to do wrong. It is willing to address sin, yet in a loving, compassionate manner. It offers hope and encouragement, without compromising God's Word.

What does this verse say is necessary in order to be able to know what God's will is?

How does it say we are to be transformed? _____

_____

WEEK SIX - FREEDOM OF THE TONGUE

If we are to renew our mind, let's look at 2 Timothy 3:16-17 to find the proper tools.

Fill in the blanks (NIV) "_____ Scripture is _____ breathed and is useful

for _____, _____, _____, and _____

in _____, so that all God's people may be _____

equipped for _____ _____ work." In order to have our minds

properly renewed, we need to fill them with God's Word. In that way, we will allow it

To have our minds properly renewed, we need to fill them with God's Word.

to teach us the things we need to know, rebuke us when we are going the wrong direction (which begins in our thought-life), correct us where our thinking is wrong, and train us in the way of righteous living. Then, we will possess everything we need to live an abundant, fruitful life that is pleasing to God, and one we all desire to live.

God is always good at confirming His Word. His desire is not that we wander in the desert; instead, He willingly shows us the way out. Philippians 4:8 is our guide into the promised land He so longs to give us. We are learning it all begins with our thought-life. Write the verse here. It, too, is one that would be beneficial to memorize.

Not every thought entering our mind is from God.

Circle the words that represent God's will for our thoughts. This is the proper filter for everything that comes into our minds. It is important to recognize that not every thought entering our mind is from God. James 3:13-18 speak of the two kinds of wisdom. Read

that passage and answer the following questions. In verse 15 what words describe

the first kind of wisdom? _____ _____ _____.

What opens the door to that kind of wisdom? _____

_____ _____ In verse 16, what does this kind of wisdom produce?

_____ and _____. Now look at verse 17.

Where does the second kind of wisdom originate? _____.

Describe that wisdom. _____

_____.What fruit does it produce?_____.

Here again, we see that our thoughts lead to either life or death.

WEEK SIX - FREEDOM OF THE TONGUE

The question remains, how do we know the origin of the wisdom? Once again, we turn to God's Word. 2 Corinthians 10:4-5 (NIV) is the tool for the job. Verse 4 tells us that "our weapons are _____ the weapons of the world. Instead they have

_____ _____ to _____ strongholds" A

stronghold is a group of thoughts that all come to the same conclusion. As each thought

is added to the group, it increases in strength, until it becomes a fortress in our minds. This scripture tells us that we have a weapon that can demolish those strongholds.

Verse 5 tells us what that weapon is, and how we use it. "We _____

arguments   and   _____   _____   that   sets   itself

up   _____   the   _____   of   _____." Now

watch carefully, because the next part tells us how we are to do this. "and we

_____ _____ EVERY _____ to make

it _____ to _____." God's Word is the filter we

use to test every thought that comes our way. If it lines up with God's Word, we receive it; if it is contrary to the Word, we throw it out immediately. WARNING: If you take that thought through your own understanding, you are in danger of accepting wrong thinking, or throwing out what God is trying to say. Let's see what Proverbs 16:25 says about this issue.

Now look up the admonishment in Proverbs 3:5

WEEK SIX - FREEDOM OF THE TONGUE

We cannot trust ourselves to judge righteously. We cannot even trust men whom we esteem righteous, to always judge rightly. We can only trust God's Word. It never fails, is always right and is always intended for our good.

Solomon was the wisest man that ever lived. Yet, with all his wisdom, he ended up going the way of the world, and lost his fervor for the things of God. He compromised with the world, making room for, and even building temples for his many wives to worship their foreign gods. In the end, he failed to fulfill his destiny. We may think we would never go that far, but sin takes us farther than we ever thought we would go, to do things we never thought we would do.

Thoughts...such little things...that in the end determine our destiny. We choose what that destiny will be...by choosing the thoughts we think.

We cannot trust ourselves to judge righteously. We can only trust God's Word.

Sin takes us farther than we ever thought we would go, to do things we never thought we would do.

106

WEEK SIX - FREEDOM OF THE TONGUE

One of the problems with a smorgasbord is that I tend to overeat. It is better to take a little at a time. Yesterday, we looked at one main serving. Let's go to the next item on the smorgasbord today.

The heart…we just can't trust it…God calls it deceitful. He doesn't just say it once, but you will find that statement in Jeremiah, Hosea and Proverbs. How can the bed of our emotions be given such a slanderous description? Let's begin by looking up Jeremiah 17: 9 and writing it here.

The heart…we just can't trust it…God calls it deceitful.

In the commentary of the New Spirit Filled Life Bible it says, "The heart is the inner self, which thinks, feels and acts. It is central to man, but it is deceitful and wicked." If that is the case, we need to take the advice given in Proverbs 4:23.

If we are going to watch over our heart with all diligence, we must fix our attention on our thought processing.

Let's go back to Jeremiah 17, and look at the first part of verse 10 (NASB). "I the Lord

search the _____, I test the _____". Do you see the connection given

again between the heart and the mind? Even in a smorgasbord, you can't get away from the connection between the heart and the mind (thoughts). If we are going to watch over our heart with all diligence, we must fix our attention on our thought processing once more. I read an article by Judah Pollack and Olivia Fox Cabane, addressing the process our mind uses to "weed the garden" of our brain. Glial cells are the gardeners; they prune our synaptic connections while we sleep. "The connections that get used less, get marked by a protein. When the microglial cells detect that mark, they bond to the protein and destroy – or prune – the synapse…you actually have some control over what your brain decides to delete while you sleep. It's the synaptic connections you don't use, that get marked for recycling. The ones you do use are the ones that get watered and oxygenated. So be mindful of what you're thinking about." (fastcompany.com; Judah Pollack and Olivia Fox Cabane/05.11.16/5:00 AM) Did you catch that last sentence? Go back and underline it. I love the way science is discovering God's Word is true.

So be mindful of what you're thinking about.

Why would it be that we don't see the gravity or seriousness of this foundational truth? Could it be as simple as choosing between walking in our emotions, compared to walking in the truth of scripture? Our emotions are neither always good, or always bad; neither do they have intellect; yet, they attempt to control our thought processing and decision making. When given the opportunity, they become powerful enough to invalidate all clear, biblical thinking. Turn to 2 Corinthians 10:3-4 (NASB)

Underline where we walk. Now circle where we DO NOT war. What do we do with

our mighty weapons? Do you see that we are destroying strongholds and fortresses?

_____ The way we destroy speculations is found in verse 5: "we are taking every

_____ captive to the obedience of Christ." Write Colossians 3:2 here:

Our emotions (fleshly part of us), focus on earthly things. Romans 8: 5-8 (NASB) speak to this. Verse 5 says that those who walk according to the flesh (allowing

their emotions to rule), set their _____ on the things of the flesh

(those things that appeal to our emotions). Verse 6 says the _____ set on

the flesh is _____., while the mind set on the Spirit is _____ and

_____. Verse 7 is a stern warning. The _____ set on the flesh is

_____ towards _____.

OUCH!!! We don't want that in our lives…but wait…there's more. "it does not

_____ itself to the _____ of _____, for it is not even able to do

so." At this point, we have a serious heart problem! Maybe it's time for a story…sometimes they help us see situations more clearly…

I t's springtime in Kansas…I love springtime. The manicured lawns are a beautiful green, the flowers are beginning to bloom, and the smell of lilacs is one of my favorite fragrances. Here in Wichita, many of the homes have sprinkler systems to help keep those lawns looking healthy and plush. On our way to church the last several weeks, just as we are approaching a stop sign, I have noticed a home with such a lawn. The sprinkler timer must be set for 7:45 am, because that's about the time we are driving through that area. All of the sprinkler jets are watering the beautiful lawn…except one. That one is watering the street…perhaps unintentionally…but definitely aimed that direction, and doing a great job. The only problem is, the grass in that area has ceased to flourish…and the street remains hard, unproductive concrete.

God speaks of our hearts becoming hardened. Ephesians 5: 26-27 speaks of how Christ loves His church. Let's write it out so we can get its full meaning.

When we refuse to allow the water of God's word to cleanse our thinking, we open ourselves up to a futile mind.

It says Christ sanctifies and washes us (His church) through His word. In doing so, He cleanses us from every spot or wrinkle, so that we will be holy and blameless before Him. What would happen if we positioned ourselves differently, so the word no longer watered us? We could become like that concrete road…hard and unproductive.

Ephesians 4: 17-19 warns us of the consequences we would incur. Let's use the NASB once more to fill in the blanks: "This I say therefore, and affirms together with the Lord that you _____ _____ _____ just as the _____ also walk, in the _____ of their _____, being _____ in their _____, excluded from the life of God, because of the _____ that is in them, because of the _____ of their _____; and they, having become _____, have given themselves over to _____, for the practice of every kind of _____ with greediness." According to this passage, describe the Gentiles' (world's) thinking:

_____

_____, Is that something desirable? _____. When we refuse to allow the water of God's word to cleanse our thinking, we open ourselves up

to a futile mind that gives itself over to sensuality (allowing emotions to dictate). Our hearts become hardened, and we find ourselves doing things we never thought possible…every kind of impurity with greediness.

I am sure the homeowners do not intend to water the street. I plan to knock on their door and let them know what they are unintentionally doing. The same goes for us… we usually don't intend to water the wrong thoughts, causing our hearts to become dry and hard. The enemy of our souls is pretty crafty. I Peter 5:8 instructs us about that.

Verse 9 says we are to resist him, firm in our faith; however, for our faith to grow and be firm, it must be watered. Let's look up one final verse for today. Proverbs 8: 32-36. Write verse 34 here:

If we want to be watered, we need to be in the right position. May we deliberately place our hearts under the fountain of God's Holy Word, and intentionally guard our minds to benefit and not destroy.

The homeowner did not intentionally direct the sprinkler jet away from his lawn, and onto the concrete. In the same way, we would never want to see our mouth used as a weapon of destruction…unless it would be directed by the Holy Spirit against God's enemy. Unfortunately, however, the enemy has been very crafty in giving us phrases that ignorantly project death into our atmosphere. Perhaps our smorgasbord choice today would be our words. We will see today that our words have the ability to heal, yet they also possess the power to destroy.

Take a quick peek at one of the first scriptures on Day One. Proverbs 18:21 is worth looking at one more time…

We have opportunity to partner with God, to bring His will into the earth realm.

We have to ask ourselves, "Does God really mean that, or is He trying to say something else?" It doesn't take long to answer that question, in view of all the other scriptures we have seen through this study. If He said it, He means it. What do you think the last part of that verse means?

Galatians 6:7 says it another way. Let's look it up and write it here.

Verse 8 gets even more explicit. It would be beneficial to read, and ponder what it says.

My desire for this study is that we would not browse over the lessons. When we do that, we are in danger of becoming like the person standing by the side of the road in Mark 4:15 (NIV) "Some people are like the seed along the path, where the word is sown. As soon as they hear it, Satan comes and takes away the word that was sown in them." Instead, we should be like the prepared ground in verse 20, that allows the word to produce an abundant harvest. Today's lesson is extremely important. When we recognize the power our words possess, we then have opportunity to partner with God, to actually bring His will into the earth realm. What a privilege… not one to be taken lightly…

Week Six - Freedom of the Tongue

I love Proverbs. One little tidbit to share…there are 31 chapters in the book of Proverbs. There are also 30-31 days in 11 of the months of the year. That presents a beautiful opportunity to read one chapter each day of the month. Proverbs possesses so much wisdom…what a marvelous opportunity to constantly be filling our minds with God's wisdom. Do you suppose God had that in mind when He organized it that way?... just a thought.

We're going to take advantage of that wisdom packed book. Let's begin in Chapter 10 (NASB). There are so many to choose from, so I'm going to pick parts of verses, in order to not bog us down. Fill in the blanks:

Proverbs 10: 19-21 When there are many _____, _____ is unavoidable, but he who _____ his _____ is wise. The _____ of the righteous is as choice silver, the _____ of the wicked is worth little. The _____ of the _____ feed many, but the _____ die for lack of _____.

Proverbs 12:13a – An evil man is _____ by the transgression of his _____

Proverbs 12:14a – A man will be _____ with good by the _____ of his _____.

Proverbs 12:18b – But the _____ of the wise brings _____.

Proverbs 12:25 – Anxiety in the _____ of a man weighs it down, but a _____ _____ makes it _____.

Proverbs 13: 2a – From the fruit of a man's _____ he enjoys good.

Verse 3 – The one who _____ his _____ preserves his life; the one who _____ wide his _____ comes to ruin.

Proverbs 16: 24 - _____ _____ are a honeycomb, sweet to the _____ and _____ to the _____.

Proverbs 18: 6 & 7 – A _____ _____ bring _____, and his _____ calls for blows. A _____ _____ is his _____, and his _____ are the _____ of his _____.

WEEK SIX - FREEDOM OF THE TONGUE

WOW! That says a lot about the power behind our words. The unrighteous mouth produces transgressions, lies in wait for blood, ensnares its owner, comes to ruin, causes strife, and is a snare to his soul. The mouth of the righteous feeds many, satisfies his soul, produces healing, makes his heart glad, enjoys good, preserves his life, and brings healing to the bones of the hearer. We are given the choice, and that choice is in the power of our tongue.

Ephesians is a good book to lead us in the right direction. Let's turn to Ephesians 4:15. Write that verse here.

We are given the choice, and that choice is in the power of our tongue.

God hates flattery (Proverbs 29:5). He says it actually spreads a net for the person's feet. Instead, He asks us to help each other grow up in Christ. We do that by speaking the truth; but if we don't use love, we simply become a noisy gong. Ephesians 4:25 echoes the same words.

Ephesians 4: 29-32 is one of my favorite bible passages. If we would put this to memory, and commit to obey what it says, we would find ourselves continually walking in the love of Christ.

Writing is a necessary step to get the truth deep into our souls. Look at verse 29. What kind of words does God tell us to speak? _____

_____ What kind are we

NOT TO SPEAK? _____ Can you see they would produce the opposite effect? _____ What would those unwholesome, corrupt words do (verse 30)? _____ We need to recognize how serious this would be…we spoke earlier in our study about the fear of God. We need to have that fear in place as we continue in verses 31 and 32. What does God command us to let go of? _____

_____ How does He tell us to treat others? _____

_____

WEEK SIX - FREEDOM OF THE TONGUE

We learned we can tell what's in our heart by what proceeds from our mouth. Listen this week to how you speak TO others, and just as importantly, what you say ABOUT others.

We have heard a lot about the power behind spoken words. We see that we can speak life, and see life happen, or we can speak death, and see death happen. I challenge you to recognize the clichés we have adopted into our vocabulary, without even noticing what they mean. Who really wants these examples to come true? "That tickles me to death…That just kills me…I love you to death…That blows my mind." What about the words we speak to those under our care? "You'll never amount to anything…She'll never change…He can't do anything right. You're so stupid." The enemy is crafty. We are warned in I Peter 5:8 to be sober, and on the alert…we have an enemy whose aim is to devour.

We can speak life, and see life happen, or we can speak death, and see death happen.

Life and death are in the power of the tongue. May you choose life…

WEEK SIX - FREEDOM OF THE TONGUE

It's time to put the finishing touches on our smorgasbord. A good meal usually ends with dessert; however, a good lesson ends with practical illustrations. That's what today's lesson is all about. We are going to look at three practical life applications. How does this all work with our words, thought processing, and heart? This study was never intended to be a series of truths that end with a signed diploma, one that is worthless in everyday life. This lesson is perhaps the most intense one in our study; however, it is also one of the most important.

SECTION ONE – This is a recap from our lesson in Job 22: 23-25. Since our heart is so important to God, it's always good to have reminders along the way. Where do we lay

our gold? _____. What (Who) do we pick

up as our gold? _____. Where is your heart today? Just a

friendly reminder…heart checks are always good.

Our choices play a large part in what comes our way.

SECTION TWO – We learned that our words hold the power of life and death. Let's look at this truth from both sides – when we speak, and when we are the recipients of those words. If we can decree something and it is established, that is true of others. Many of us have been victims of verbal abuse from those over us, either during childhood, or currently today. Sometimes parents or teachers, because of wounds in their own lives, victimize those under them with hurtful, wounding words. Those decrees can follow us throughout our adulthood, and even be transferred to our children after us if they are not addressed. We are going to look closely at Isaiah 54:17 and allow the Holy Spirit to speak to us through His Word.

I love the different translations, but for simplicity's sake, let's continue with the NASB. Write the verse here so we can examine it together:

The first part of this verse is a very familiar one. If we read that section out of context, we develop an inappropriate view that no weapon the enemy sends our way would ever harm us. Life lessons prove that mindset to be invalid. This is definitely God's will for our lives; however, as we have learned, our choices play a large part in what comes our way. We remember that Deuteronomy 30:19 says God honors our choice of either life or death. If God would force any one particular choice on us, it would be that all people would go to heaven. 2 Peter 3:9 tells us, "The Lord…is patient toward you, not wishing for any to perish, but for all to come to repentance." Yet, we know that many people will be in hell, because they did not choose to repent and accept Jesus as Lord of their lives. In the same way, it is not God's will for any weapon formed against us to succeed. In fact, He continues on in that verse, to show us how we can prevent that from happening. (Of course, without the verses in Job, where we surrender to God as the Lord of our lives, we invalidate this promise, as well as many others. We also need to be open to the Holy Spirit's conviction if there are areas in our lives that need repentance.)

Let's continue on in verse 17 to see what OUR part is in this proclamation. It declares that every tongue that accuses us in judgment should be condemned; however, who

is the one responsible to condemn that tongue? _____. What if you don't do

that? _____. Looking further, what gives you the right to do

that? _____ I looked up the defini-

tion of heritage: "something that comes or belongs to one, by reason of birth or legal descent." 1 John 3:1 calls us "children of God". This verse calls us servants, and says this is our inheritance. It gives us the right to condemn every tongue that would accuse us. I like the fact that it calls it a tongue. To me, that is referring to the source, not just the words spoken. The definition of condemn is "to pronounce to be guilty; to judge or pronounce to be unfit for use or service". When I condemn that tongue, I pronounce that it will bear no fruit, and any previous fruit is destroyed in Jesus' Name. In the last part of the verse, God states that our vindication is from Him. If we will confront and condemn those words, He will vindicate us. I love that!

Now, let's put that in practice. No one can hurt or wound us with their words. They can give us **opportunity** to be hurt or wounded, but it is actually **our choice** if we decide to be hurt. There is a real temptation that comes with those words…sometimes "hurt feels good". We like to tell everyone how hurt and wounded we are…then, if they feel sorry for us, it feeds that sick part of hurt, and justifies our woundedness, enticing us to remain in that state of mind. The same is true of unforgiveness…no matter what happens, we are the one that chooses whether to forgive or remain bitter. With that said, let me draw you a mental picture…

When someone says something cruel to you, you have a few choices to make. First of all, you have the choice to receive those words into your soul and become hurt, or you can condemn them and disarm their power. YOU FORGIVE THE ONE WHO SPOKE THE WORDS, WHILE AT THE SAME TIME CONDEMNING THE WORDS. That leads to life.

Another choice available is to accept the words, and allow them to wound you. That opens you up to a victim spirit, who will then open the door for others…adding to the woundedness in your life. Eventually, you will be so wrapped up in yourself and your emotions that you will be of no use to the Kingdom of God. You will fall into the description of one who has chosen to be a vessel of dishonor, full of bitterness, anger, and self-pity… not a very pretty picture…but still your choice.

After you have condemned the words spoken, and forgiven the speaker, there is one more choice you can make. This is an "EXTRA CREDIT" possibility. Turn to Luke 6:27-28 and write them here.

They can give us opportunity to be hurt or wounded, but it is actually our choice if we decide to be hurt.

No matter what happens, we are the one that chooses whether to forgive or remain bitter.

It would be easy to pick up those words, and hurl them back to the speaker; however, God is giving you an opportunity to go the extra mile. He is asking you to love, and do good to those who hate you, bless those who curse you, and pray for those who mistreat you. The question comes to mind, "How do I bless those who curse me?" The answer is pretty straightforward. You don't pretend. Remember, God hates flattery. Instead, take the blessing to a higher level. Ask God to open their eyes to their need for Him - that they might recognize His love for them, repent and be saved. Ask Him to supply their deepest needs. That takes it out of what they did to you personally, and sets it in the eternal realm. It also qualifies you for the reward in verses 36-38. It would be good to read those, and take them to heart.

SECTION THREE – We have come full circle to our thought-life. Remember, as a man thinks in his heart, so he is (Proverbs 23:7). We're going to begin with a scripture that doesn't seem to fit into this picture, but looking closer we will discover a great truth.

Ask God to open their eyes to their need for Him.

The scripture, Ephesians 4:28 (NASB) begins, "Let him who steals _____

_____ _____. If we have a problem with stealing, we easily see that we need to stop stealing. However, "not stealing" is not the opposite of "stealing". It simply takes us to neutral. We have stopped doing something that is wrong. We have not begun doing anything right; we have simply brought ourselves to a neutral point. Over time, our mind and emotions are trained by our actions. If we have been in the habit of stealing, our THOUGHT PROCESSING AND OUR EMOTIONS have been trained to view stealing as the easiest and most familiar option. If we only get to "neutral" without going any further, we will soon default back to "stealing". We can't stop at this point…we must continue. So let's look at the scripture again. "Let him who steals steal no longer;

but rather let him _____. The next step to our freedom is that, instead of

stealing, we begin to labor with our own hands. However, "labor" is still not the opposite of "stealing". We will find that labor is hard work…much harder than stealing…and since our mind and emotions have been trained to steal, not only are we battling an enemy who is trying to convince us to go back to stealing, we are ALSO BATTLING OUR OWN MIND AND EMOTIONS. If we only go this far on our journey, we will eventually go back to stealing. It is familiar, our thought processing and emotions are trained to go there, and we have an enemy who will give us many opportunities to do so. Stay with me; we only have one more step to go! "Let him who steals, steal no longer; but rather let him labor, performing with his own hands what is good, in order that he may have

something to _____ to him who has need." If we are laboring just to labor, we

will get tired and give up. If our FOCUS is on laboring, it will become too hard. BUT, if

we labor IN ORDER THAT WE MAY GIVE, our entire focus and motivation has changed. Now we are laboring IN ORDER THAT WE MAY GIVE. "Giving" is the opposite of "stealing". GIVING IS WALKING IN BREAKTHROUGH.

That applies to stealing, but how can we use this to apply to other issues in our lives? The question we must ask ourselves is this: "What pointed us in the direction of either stealing or giving?" Finding the key to that question will give us the key to other areas in our lives.

Remember, we have learned God gives us the choice of life or death, blessing or curse. I believe the answer depends almost entirely upon the **MINDSET** we choose. If we choose a godly mindset, we will be willing to endure any necessary hardship involved. If we choose death, we will live a self-absorbed, critical life. Let's see Jesus' response to this in Hebrews 12:2:

Our actions are determined by the choices we make in our mind.

The joy set before Him (GIVING His life for our salvation), was worth the horrific hard labor on His part. He had already determined in his mind what His choice would be. In the same way, our actions are determined by the choices we make in our mind. We need to make a conscious decision that the victory of success is worth the "labor" necessary to change.

Negative thoughts lead to negative decisions: bitterness, selfishness, impatience, concentrating on the faults of others…all death producers…all an abomination to God.

Life-giving thoughts lead to life-giving decisions: compassion, unselfish acts, patience, making an allowance for one another's faults while concentrating on their positive attributes…all giving life…all pure gold in the eyes of God.

Negative thoughts lead to negative decisions.

One last scripture: II Corinthians 10:5

Life-giving thoughts lead to life-giving decisions.

Circle the two things we are destroying. How does it say we are going to do that?

_____ Remember, it's not

enough just to stop "stealing"…the victory is in the "giving". It's not enough to stop thinking negative thoughts…the victory is in replacing them with life-giving thoughts. Philippians 4:8 is a wonderful guideline to follow. Summarize that verse here:

PROVERBS 23:7 "AS A MAN THINKS IN HIS HEART, SO HE IS." Life or death…the choice belongs to me for my life…and you for yours.

Life…what a great choice…what a wonderful way to live!!!

FREEDOM THROUGH THE HOLY SPIRIT

John 8:31, 32 As we _____ in God's word, we find the

_____ that sets us free.

John 16: 13, 14 The _____ _____ guides us into all the truth.

I Corinthians 2:9-13 God's Spirit reveals all that _____ freely gives us.

DO WE ALREADY HAVE THE HOLY SPIRIT?

John 3: 3, 5 Unless you are born of _____ and the _____,

you cannot enter into the kingdom of God.

When we accept Jesus as Lord and Savior, His _____ lives in us.

IS THAT ENOUGH?

Acts 1:4, 5 Jesus told the disciples to wait for the _____ of the Holy

Spirit.

The Holy Spirit gives us _____ to be witnesses for Jesus.

Luke 11:13 Our Father gives the Holy Spirit to those who _____.

II Corinthians 3:17, 18 Where the Spirit of the Lord is, there is

_____.

WEEK SEVEN - FREEDOM THROUGH THE HOLY SPIRIT

Without Baptism of Holy Spirit, we can still be lead into the truth; however, there Is not as much freedom as when we've surrendered totally to Him.

Romans 8:26, 27 When we don't know how to pray, the Holy Spirit

_____ for us according to the _____ of God.

DIFFERENCE BETWEEN SPIRITUAL GIFTS FOR THE BODY AND INDIVIDUAL GIFTS

1 Corinthians 12: 7 The gifts of the Spirit are for the _____ good.

Mark 16: 17-18; 1 Corinthians 12: 4-11; 14: 1 In the church body, everyone does not walk in every office; however, as an individual, the Holy Spirit offers the ability for any disciple to heal, deliver, speak with a new tongue, and prophecy, among other things.

Ezekiel 47: How deep are you willing to go?

Ankle Deep _____ Knee Deep _____ Waist Deep _____ All The Way _____

You can receive the Holy Spirit simply by asking God for it in the quiet of your heart. Or you may desire to have someone pray for you or with you. It won't necessarily be an emotional experience.

You can get by without the Holy Spirit, but you can get by without two legs also. Given the choice, very few people would do without their legs. When someone loses a leg, he gets an artificial substitute. Don't substitute your pride where the Holy Spirit should be!

NOTES:

The Holy Spirit has become my most intimate Friend. I am excited for the opportunity to introduce you to Him. Perhaps you already know Him…perhaps you know Him from afar. There was a time in my life I had no knowledge He even existed. I don't know how I even functioned during those days…in fact, looking back, I realize my life was incomplete and in shambles without Him. I'm so glad He came and made Himself known to me.

The bible is full of references to the Holy Spirit. God was gracious to me by moving a lady into our farming community, who began a bible study and invited me to attend. As I began to study God's Word, I became intensely hungry for the life I found inside its pages. As I ravenously read the truths it contained, God was true to His Word. I found the truth, and it set me free! Journeying with me on my voyage to truth was my precious friend, Margaret. I remember the day we realized the life-giving truth, and accepted the Lordship of Jesus into our lives…but even more awaited us…so much more!

Looking back, I realize my life was incomplete and in shambles without Him.

Margaret's friends were writing to her about the Holy Spirit and the power they had discovered. Turn to Acts 1:8 and write it here.

Jesus was telling this to His disciples just before He was taken up into heaven. Let's set the background for this statement. First, look at Jesus' conversation with Nicodemus in John 3:1-7. Jesus is explaining to him the necessary step to change citizenship from the world's system into the Kingdom of God. We discussed this earlier in our lessons, but Colossians 1:12-14 tells us that, what Jesus did on the cross, made it possible for God to deliver us from Satan's kingdom and establish us in the Kingdom of God. Here in His conversation with Nicodemus, Jesus is telling what is necessary to make the transfer. Paraphrase John 3:5 here:

Verse 6 explains the two types of birth…flesh and Spirit.

WEEK SEVEN - FREEDOM THROUGH THE HOLY SPIRIT

The world had not yet experienced their Savior at this point. Jesus had not died, taking our sins to the cross. The promise was there, but had not yet been fulfilled. However, in John 20:22, when Jesus was speaking to His disciples, it was after the crucifixion and resurrection. The promise had been fulfilled. Jesus is giving His disciples an opportunity to receive what He had promised over and over to them. Write the verse here:

If our lives don't exemplify Him, our words lack any type of validity.

I have taken pains to show you this, so you can get a clear picture of Jesus' statement to His disciples in Acts 1:8 above. Paraphrase Jesus' words in Acts 1:4-5 here:

He is speaking to His disciples who already had received the Holy Spirit; yet, He is telling them to wait until they are BAPTIZED with the Holy Spirit. What did He promise them they would receive once that happened? _____ What would that power give them the ability to do? _____

_____ Sometimes it is easy to talk about Jesus to others but the proof is in the pudding. If our lives don't exemplify Him, our words lack any type of validity. However, if others see us living a life of freedom, joy and purity, our words are receivable and possess the power to draw others to the life-giving truth we ourselves have found.

God promises to give us everything we need to live a godly life. 2 Peter 1:3 is an important verse to remember. Write it here:

How does it say we receive those promises? _____

_____

Check out 1 Corinthians 2:12. Write it here:

What does the Holy Spirit reveal to us? _____

_____ Checking back to 2 Peter, let's look at 1:4. What does God say His promises

would enable us to do? _____

_____ That certainly sounds like

God is promising power to successfully live a life full of power, love, and purity. One last scripture for this section. Let's look at 2 Corinthians 5:17-20. What type of ministry

has God ordained for each of us? _____ What

title does He give us? _____ An ambassador doesn't represent

himself – he represents the one who appoints him. God has appointed each of us to

be His ambassador to others on the earth. What is our mission? _____

_____

The one who sends an ambassador to represent him, expects that person to think and

act like the one sending him. Jesus said in Acts 1:8, when we receive the baptism of the Holy Spirit, we will be empowered to be His witnesses. Those are His words…which means He knows what we need.

When we receive the baptism of the Holy Spirit, we will be empowered to be His witnesses.

I would have wiped out a long time ago if God had left me to my own way. Don't let what you don't know, keep you from receiving God's power in your life.

When my friend, Margaret told me about the Holy Spirit, I really didn't think I needed Him in my life…after all, I had accepted Jesus and all was good. That could have kept me from receiving the power I would need to overcome strongholds the enemy had built into my life…he intended destruction, for both me and my children after me. Jesus told His disciples, who had already received the Holy Spirit, that they should wait in Jerusalem until they received power from on high. Fortunately, God in His mercy, didn't leave me there. I remember the phone conversation…deciding Margaret needed Him and I didn't. When I hung up the phone, a still small voice asked, "What if I wanted to give this to you?" Recognizing that Voice, I simply said, "If You want to give that to me, I want it." The power I received in that moment was not an emotional feeling, or even anything I understood. However, in the next weeks and months, His truth became a reality to me. Looking back, I realize I would have wiped out a long time ago if God had left me to my own way. He knew what I needed. We'll look into this further tomorrow. In the meantime, don't let what you don't know, keep you from receiving God's power in your life…everything we need pertaining to life and godliness…partakers of the divine nature…all because He loves us. What a God!!!

WEEK SEVEN - FREEDOM THROUGH THE HOLY SPIRIT

Truth – what a powerful tool. When we know the truth we can base our every life's decision on it. Of course, knowing the truth about mathematical equations won't help us in the area of history…or knowing how to diagram a sentence isn't the truth we need to understand chemistry. The truth we need at the moment needs to be the right truth…so how do we tap into that kind of relevant truth in every situation? To answer that question, let's go back to 2 Peter 1:3. (NSAB) What truth do we find in

this text? "_____ pertaining to _____ and _____." How

do we find that? "Through the _____ _____ of

_____ who called us by His own glory and excellence." I can't promise you an

Since God created
the universe and
everything in it,
He can maneuver
us through each
circumstance life
hands us.

'A' in math, or a high level position as a medical researcher if you study the bible every day. I can't even promise you a good review as an author…there are books you can read and people you can listen to that will help you in those areas. There are, however, promises we have already seen that offer clear guidance in each area, through obedience to God's word. Psalm 81:13-16 gives us good advice. What does God say He will

do if we listen to Him and walk in His ways? _____

_____ Since God is the one

who created the universe and everything in it, it would make sense He is the one who can maneuver us through each circumstance life hands us. Perhaps He is the one we need to turn to for those math questions after all! Of course, it would be foolish for us to expect to excel in that subject, if we have not spent any time studying in that area. In the same way, it would be foolish for us to think we can know all the things God offers us, if we haven't taken time to study them.

Let's begin today in 1 Corinthians 2: 9-12. Paraphrase verse 9

Who has He prepared these things for? _____.

Who does verse 10 say will reveal these things to us? _____. Why

does verse 10 & 11 say the Spirit will know these things? _____

_____. Paul is talking to Christians. If we have received Jesus as

Lord, whose spirit does this say we have abiding in us? _____

Because of that, what do we know? _____

With that in mind, let's take a slight rabbit trail, and look at a few familiar verses.

When we find ourselves in a fearful situation, 2 Timothy 1:7 says, "God has NOT given us _____, but He HAS given us _____, _____ and _____ _____", Instead of caving in to fear, we need to use our sound mind in the situation. What does James 1:5 tell us to do if we lack wisdom? _____. How will God respond? _____. It goes on to say that when we ask,

If we do our part, we can trust God to do His.

we should ask in faith and not doubt. Again, that's our part. If we do our part, we can trust God to do His. Philippians 4:6-7 tells us what to do if we become anxious. _____. What will God give? _____ _____. It doesn't say God will answer us the way we want Him to; however, He promises peace beyond our understanding, which comes from trusting Him to do the right thing. If we are struggling with unforgiveness, what does Ephesians 4:31-32 say we should do? _____

These are simple examples, but can be applied to many circumstances of life. In John 14:26, Jesus tells His disciples the Holy Spirit will _____ _____ and _____. If He is going to remind us of things He has said, it makes sense we need to have heard them (or read them) previously. That's our part…it is the Holy Spirit's part to remind us. He also said He would teach us all things. We need to be listening intently for His voice.

Look at John 16:12-14. Jesus had so much He wanted to share with the disciples, but He knew they wouldn't be able to comprehend it all. Only after the resurrection would they be able to fully understand what was taking place. In verse 13, Jesus calls Him the Sprit of _____. Whose words will He speak to us? _____. Who will He glorify? _____. In fact, 1 Corinthians 12: 3 states that no one can confess Jesus is Lord without the Holy Spirit revealing it to them. The Holy Spirit simply wants to unveil Jesus in all His fullness. His Spirit is the very essence of Him, and deserves the same honor, glory, and praise.

Check out 2 Corinthians 3:17:

This places the Holy Spirit in the same preeminence as Jesus the Son, and God the Father. It also tells us that wherever He reigns, He brings freedom. I can't think of a better reason to surrender and desire as much of the Holy Spirit as is available. Ephesians 5:18 instructs us to be filled with the Spirit. The more we surrender to God, the greater the capacity we have to be filled with His Spirit…and enjoy the freedom that follows.

The more we surrender to God's Spirit, the more freedom we will enjoy.

Look up Galatians 5:1 and write it here:

We are encouraged to stand firm in the freedom that Christ paid for…and where the Spirit of the Lord is, there is freedom…sounds to me like these two scriptures go hand in hand. The more we surrender to God's Spirit, the more freedom we will enjoy.

I think I'll have a cup of Freedom – Mmmm…It Tastes So Good!!!

WEEK SEVEN - FREEDOM THROUGH THE HOLY SPIRIT

Have you ever come to a fork in the road and you don't know which one to take? That is my dilemma today. There are two roads I want to take, but am in a quandary which one to take first. Perhaps we should go down one side and then, if time permits, come back and try the other one. Sounds kind of fun...come join me...

There are so many assumptions about the Holy Spirit. Many of those assumptions have split churches. It is interesting to me that other major doctrines find their place within the church body, but this one is declared divisive. It would seem that God's archenemy is deathly afraid of the church embracing the power behind the fullness of God's presence. In fact, he has called an all-out war to fight against this. Perhaps we should get out our compass – God's Word – and see what He has to say. Then we can make our decision based on the Word of God, and not on what we may have heard from others, or assumptions we have made.

God's archenemy is deathly afraid of the church embracing the power behind the fullness of God's presence.

The first road we'll take begins with Galatians 5:22-23. Matthew 7:16 and Luke 6:44 tell us we will be known by our fruit. If that is the case, let's see what kind of fruit is evident with the Holy Spirit. Write the nine fruits of the Spirit listed in Galatians.

_____, _____, _____, _____, _____,

_____, _____, _____, _____.

Are any of those fruits offensive to you? _____ Are there any that you would not

want? If so list them here and explain why

Next, look up James 1:17. It tells us the kind of gifts God gives. What two words are used

to describe those gifts? _____ and _____. Remember, yester-

day we discovered that the Lord is the Spirit, so these words could also be used to describe the gifts the Spirit gives. With that in mind, let's turn to 1 Corinthians 12: 4-11. The first three verses here tell us Who is the giver of the gifts, ministries and effects. It

is interesting that they include three words to describe the Giver – and those words

make up the Trinity. Write those three words here: _____, _____,

_____. In the same way that God the Father, God the Son, and God the Holy

Spirit are one, Their desire is that we, with our many gifts, would also be one. Also, note that in the next five verses they simply refer to the giver as the Spirit...no jealousy or

self-promotion...simply the Three in One. What is the reason given in verse 7 for these

manifestations? _____.

Sometimes we mistakenly think that a person's gifts are because of their holiness, or somehow connected to their value. This should correct that false concept. It should also speak to each of us. If we are not allowing the Holy Spirit to move through the gifts He desires to give us, we are hurting the Body of Christ, which is selfish and harmful to the rest of the Body.

There is another false concept that needs to be discussed. Sometimes we put more value on one gift or ministry than on other seemingly less powerful ones. How do

verses 12-25 address this? _____

_____ What does verse 25 say the end result should be? _____.

_____. This brings up another point we need to

address. Looking over these verses, are there any gifts or ministries that you do not

want or would refuse? If so, write them here. _____.

According to verse 11, who is the One who decides which gifts to give to whom?

_____ Realizing the gifts are given by the Holy Spirit, and

they are not for you but for the Body, are you willing to change your mind?

_____

Well, we're at the end of this road. Tomorrow we'll take the other path...I think we have enough to think about for today...maybe some decisions to make.

If we are not allowing the Holy Spirit to move through the gifts He desires to give us, we are hurting the Body of Christ.

Here we are at that same fork in the road…ready to see where the other path leads. In Ezekiel 47, he sees a river progressively getting deeper. In the beginning it is simply up to his ankles, then to his knees, then waist, and finally it was too deep to cross. At that point, if you were going to enter the river, you would simply have to jump in and try to swim. One thing Ezekiel realized as he surveyed the river was that "everything lives where the river goes".

God has a river He is inviting you to enter. He is also giving you the freedom to choose where you enter. If you enter in at ankle depth, the world will still love you…a little bit of religion is still acceptable, even today. If you choose knee deep, you will be looked upon as a little weird but will, for the most part, still be acceptable. Waist deep presents a problem. You are looking way too much like a child of God at this point, and the world will have a problem handling your convictions. You will be excluded from many functions, and even overlooked concerning many promotions; however, you can still find a place among many other like-minded people. I must warn you, however…if you choose to jump in where the water is deep, there is a current waiting for you and you will not be able to choose where the river will take you. You will have to abandon yourself, not to the mercy of the river…but to the Creator of the river. The only reason you would want to jump in at this point is because you see what Ezekiel saw…"everything will live where the river goes". You will be a part of a life-giving stream, giving hope to a hopeless world.

If you choose to jump in where the water is deep, You will have to abandon yourself, not to the mercy of the river…but to the Creator of the river.

You will be a part of a life-giving stream, giving hope to a hopeless world.

The apostles entered that stream. We read about them in the book of Acts. At the end of the gospels, they were simply followers of Jesus. Read John 21:3. What does

Peter decide to do? _____ How many disciples join him? (Verse 2)

_____ So Peter decided to go back to his fishing, and six other disciples went

with him. Yet in Acts 2, after the Holy Spirit fell, it was Peter who stood in front of the multitude, proclaiming the Good News with mighty power. Look at Acts 2:41. How

many people were saved that day? _____ That was the beginning of a power

packed legacy we now read about with awe.

Come with me as I share about two areas I consider extremely important. They may be new to you, but please listen with an open heart and mind. I love what the Berean

church did in Acts 17:11 (NASB) where they were "examining the _____

_____, to see whether _____ _____ were so". Let's begin

in 1 Corinthians 12:27-31. I will attempt to clear up some confusion between the "individual gifts" and the "Body gifts" (gifts used during assembling together as a body). Those are simply my words for them…you can change them however you wish. I chose them from verse 27 where it says we are Christ's body, and individually members of it. In verse 7 we find the words, "manifestation of the Spirit for the common good", that is then identified in verses 8-11. In verse 28 it then begins to list the "appointments in the church". Concerning these appointments, in verses 29-30 it asks the questions, "are all apostles, prophets, teachers…etc"? The answer given is "no".

I believe the confusion lies in who Paul is speaking to in each case. As an appointment in the church, God has appointed some as prophets; yet what does Paul encourage everyone individually to desire to do in 1 Corinthians 14:1? _____

_____. If we are not able to prophecy, then Paul is asking us to desire something

we can never attain…God would be dangling a carrot in front of us that we could never reach. That is contrary to God's character. Verse 30 goes on to say that all do not have the gifts of healing; yet look up Mark 16:17-18. What will believers do in Jesus name?

Again, God would be contrary to His Word if we are not able to pray successfully for the sick. The very same thing is true of speaking in tongues. Check out 1 Corinthians 14:4. At first it looks like Paul is putting down anyone who speaks in a tongue.

What does he say about one who prophesies? _____.

If speaking in tongues does not edify the church, why would God give it to anyone? Let's take a closer look and see if we're missing something. What does speaking in

tongues do for the person? _____ Edify means to build up.

Frankly, if I am not "built up", I am not much use to anyone else. Look at verse 18 and

write what Paul is saying here _____

_____. Wait a minute – if Paul is

glad he speaks in tongues, surely he isn't meaning that it is wrong to do so. To get the proper perspective, read verse 19. Oh! IN THE CHURCH (for the edification of the church) perhaps I need to go back and read verse 5. Who does Paul wish would speak

in tongues? _____. Read further in that verse. One who prophesies is

greater UNLESS what? _____ So that the

_____ is edified. Also, in verse 2, who does it say we are speaking to if

we are speaking in a tongue? _____. That doesn't sound like it would be

such a bad thing…right?

Here is my take on all of this. There are personal gifts and there are gifts for the Body.

Both are great tools/gifts given by our good, good Father for our benefit. If I am all by myself, or with a few like-minded believers, I am encouraged to use these "manifestations of the Spirit" for my edification and for the common good of those around me. If someone is sick, I can lay hands on them and pray for them. The same is true if they need deliverance. I am also encouraged to prophesy (taking the word I hear God speaking to me and sharing it with its intended recipient). I can use the tongue God has given me as a prayer language, where I speak to Him mysteries only He understands…that also edifies me so I can function as an encourager to the Body in whatever way I am needed. I can operate with the gift of discernment, word of wisdom, word of knowledge or any other manifestation the Lord deems right and/or necessary for me to possess. All of this aids in receiving all I need for life and godliness, according to 2 Peter 1.

There are personal gifts and there are gifts for the Body.

There are also appointments given to edify the church. Reading 1 Corinthians 14: 20, what are we instructed to do?

As we look at all of this as mature believers, verses 26-33 become a good guideline. Write verse 26 here:

Lots to think about…lots to pray about…lots to search the scriptures to see what God says…

There are members of the Body that God has appointed as prophets, others with gifts of healing, administration, teaching, etc. (1 Corinthians 12:28) As it says, let it all be done for edification for the individual members present. Lots to think about…lots to pray about…lots to search the scriptures to see what God says… Let's take today and tomorrow and do just that.

Everywhere the river flowed there was life…we can read about that river or we can jump in with both feet…I think I'm ready for a swim!

Mark 16:17 - Those Who Believe Will Cast Out _____.

WHAT DO DEMONS DO?

Matthew 8:28 -Demons are _____

Mark 5:1-7 - Demons are _____ and have

_____ strength.

Matthew 12:22 - Demons can cause _____ and

_____

Luke 13:11 - Demons can cause _____.

Matthew 15:22 *Demons can trouble* _____ *as well as adults.*

Jesus freed them <u>all</u> - bodies and minds

WHAT DOES JESUS SAY WE SHOULD DO?

Mark 9:43-47 - Get rid of whatever causes you to _____.

Matthew 12:28-31 - First, _____the strong man; then cast them out by

the _____ of God;

THEN WHAT?

Matthew 12:43-45 - If you simply cast out the demon but don't fill that spot with the Holy Spirit, it will _____ and bring _____. with it.

NOTES:

We need to start with a story – maybe even two…we'll see. These lessons didn't develop because I lived a perfect, carefree life and wanted others to be able to have the same lifestyle I enjoyed. They have come out of God's answer to a desperate cry from the heart of a young woman, who found herself entrapped in a cruel, life-sucking, heart rendering lifestyle, with no known way of escape. That might sound over-dramatic to some of you, but it is the truth. As I share my story, please know that God has moved mightily in my life, and I have found true freedom…that is why I share what I share…I want others to find that same freedom. I have given my life to that purpose. I was so desperate…I didn't think I could ever be set free, but God heard my cry and rescued me. Psalms 18 is my story. That is why I love God so deeply…I am so grateful for His love…so grateful that He rescued me when I couldn't rescue myself. The things I share are for the benefit of the reader. I apologize if it is too much detail for some…but the story must be told.

He rescued me when I couldn't rescue myself.

My mother was one of 14 children. She was the second to the oldest daughter…and was raped repeatedly by her father. The one who should have been her protector was actually her abuser. It did terrible things to her…I wish I had known then what I know now…no one was there to walk her through to freedom. I'm glad she is with Jesus now…she truly knows how love and freedom look and feel.

Because of the type of abuse, she took on the personality that is common among that sector. She married four times and had numerous relationships in-between. She was constantly looking for love and approval, but could never find it in a human being. When I was 7 years old, she married for the fourth time and "Dad" adopted the youngest four children. My older sister had already married by that time. It would seem that all would be good from that point on, but that wasn't the case. Mother had grown to hate men, so we immediately saw this man as our enemy. On his part, he had married a woman with five dysfunctional kids and didn't know how to handle that situation. In his frustration, he became an angry, vengeful man. Life was far from pretty. There was physical abuse towards my brothers. I escaped that part, but the emotional abuse… the screaming and yelling…the word curses…were an everyday occurrence. I swore I would NEVER treat my children the way I was being treated…but I did.

I was 18 years old when I married John, my husband. I know now I married him to escape, but also because I knew he loved me, which I so desperately needed. In the beginning of our marriage, John gave 110%…and I took it all, but wanted more. That's the truth…not very pretty, but the truth (God has worked in amazing ways through the years and I now love my husband dearly and am so thankful for him). Our first daughter was born 16 ½ months after we were married. Two years later came our second daughter, and 3 years later came a son. A few months after our son was born I accepted Jesus as my Lord and Savior. I was sure all my problems would be solved and I would become the loving mother I always wanted to be. That wasn't the case. In public I was a loving, caring wife and mother. Even in my husband's presence, I was free to be that person…however, when I was alone with my children, I became another person.

WEEK EIGHT - FREEDOM FROM DEMONIC CONTROL

There was a presence that took over that I could not control. It was like I was watching another person yell and scream at those innocent children. By now, 16 months later, one more daughter was born, so my four children were now the target of an evil force I could not control.

I will always remember the day I stood in the garage of our farmhouse after sending my children after the mail. The mailbox was a distance from the house, and would give them a few minutes free from my tirades. As I stood there, I told God it would be better for my children if I were dead. I knew they would never want my God because of the way I was treating them. I also told Him I knew He had to have a better way, but if not, it would be better if I were dead. That evening, when everyone else had gone to bed, God led me in deliverance from a demon of hostility. It was the most horrible thing I had ever experienced, but as the Holy Spirit instructed me step by step, I was set free. He then told me the demon was gone, but the habit (mind-set) was still there and would have to be dealt with. We have covered some of that in the lesson on the tongue, and will cover more in future lessons. This was my first step to freedom...true freedom. That freedom wouldn't come suddenly, and it wouldn't come easily...but it came, and I have been set free. That is my story. Others have their own stories...hopefully through listening to my story, someone has found hope...lasting, beautiful hope and the promise of the possibility of freedom. Let's start our study.

That freedom wouldn't come suddenly, and it wouldn't come easily...but it came, and I have been set free.

Look at 1 Peter 5:8

Jesus says this in a rather unique way in Matthew 10:16. Fill in the blanks. "Be as

_____ as snakes and as _____ as doves." There

are definitely traps set for us by the enemy. We need to be ever mindful of that fact. Psalms 140: 4-5 speaks to the plots of the enemy. Read the verses and paraphrase what the Lord is saying.

We see that we have a real enemy whose main goal is to set traps to trip us into bondage and sin. Verses 6-8 in this Psalm offer a good declaration and prayer. Paraphrase it here:

WEEK EIGHT - FREEDOM FROM DEMONIC CONTROL

When I first became a Christian and started reading my bible, I was shocked to read about the demons. I wondered where they had gone because, in ignorance, I didn't think they were operating in the world today. I was so wrong…in fact, the very forces I denied were the ones who were working so forcefully in my own life. As my eyes were open, I came to the realization that, if they were not confronted, they would continue to reign and hold me captive. Some of Jesus' last words are recorded in Mark 16: 17-20. Write verse 17 here:

The very forces I denied were the ones who were working so forcefully in my own life.

The very first thing Jesus tells us His followers will do, is to cast out demons…interesting. He knew where our battle would lie. Record 2 Corinthians 10:3-4:

We can battle all day long in the flesh – against people and circumstances – but unless we deal with the root cause, we will constantly be battling one symptom after another, to no avail. As we read the Gospels (Matthew, Mark, Luke, and John), we discover that much of the time, Jesus was dealing with situations that required deliverance. Even physical healings were many times remedied as He dealt with the main force behind them. Let's look at a few situations. Record the type of healing through deliverance in the following verses.

Matthew 9:32-33_____ ;

Matthew 12: 22 _____ ;

Matthew 17: 14-15, 18; _____

Take time to read these verses, telling of Jesus' ministry of both healing and deliverance: Matthew 4: 23-26; Matthew 8:16; Matthew 15: 29-31; Mark 1:34; Mark 3: 10-11.

Next, let's get a glimpse of some of the things demons might be responsible for in our lives, or in the lives of others. Please note that I am not saying every one of these cases has to be caused by demonic activity. What I am saying is, if that is the case, we now have an opportunity to see that person set free. One excellent passage is Mark

5:1-7. Where was he living?: _____ Describe his symptoms: _____

WEEK EIGHT - FREEDOM FROM DEMONIC CONTROL

Some of the things I see are isolation; superhuman strength; torment; self-destructive cutting (sound familiar in today's society?). Look at Luke 13:11. What did the demon cause? _____ We already saw scriptures that describe deafness or blindness; and epilepsy...all seemingly physical issues, but sometimes demonic in nature.

One last topic for today...what about children? Can a child be influenced or tormented by a demon? To find the answer to that, let's look up two scriptures, starting

Remember what we have learned... life is a journey.

with Mark 9:17. Who was brought to Jesus for deliverance? _____.

Now look at Matthew 15:22. Who was the woman asking Jesus to deliver?

_____. What is the first scripture reference we looked up today?

_____ What did it tell us to do? _____

_____. From that passage, what does the enemy want to do?

_____ 1 Corinthians 10:13 tells us that every

He came to set the captives free.

time we are tempted to give in to evil, God offers us something. What is that?

_____. John 14:6 tells us what that "way" looks like. Write

the verse here. _____

_____. Jesus is the

way. He has paid the price for full redemption, and that redemption includes being delivered from the enemy's hands, and transferred into the kingdom where Jesus reigns. Write Colossians 1:13-14 here:

Remember what we have learned...life is a journey, but as we continue listening to the Holy Spirit, we will find the truth of Philippians 1:6

These lessons are designed to thwart the scheme's of the enemy by exposing and eliminating any legal access we would have given him. Tomorrow we will go deeper into when and how to confront that enemy. For today, I thank God that He has enclosed us behind and before, and laid His hand upon us. I also thank Him that He has covered our head in the day of battle. (Psalms 139: 5; Psalms 140: 7). I'm grateful for His words, "It is finished". (John 19: 30). I'm especially glad He came to set the captives free. (Luke 4:18).

Freedom – It Tastes So Good!!!

Years ago, I was told that the way Secret Service representatives learn to detect counterfeit bills is that they are locked in a room with real currency. As they study the real bills, they become so well acquainted with them, that they can recognize a counterfeit simply because they sense something is different, even if they don't know exactly what that "something" is. With new technology I'm sure things have changed, but the symbolism still remains. If we study the authentic item, we will be better equipped to recognize the counterfeit. Let's try that with the Holy Spirit. In our lesson on the Holy Spirit, we learned about the fruit of the Spirit. Let's go back to Galatians 5:22-23

and list again those nine qualities: _____ _____ _____

_____ _____ _____ _____ _____

_____. When we submit to the Lordship of Jesus, we should find that type of fruit flowing more and more in and through our lives. If we are honest with each other, we will admit we are a work in progress. Let's look again at 2 Corinthians 3: 17-18. What does it say will happen as we behold the Lord's glory? _____

_____. We should be able to look within and realize we are becoming more and more transformed into the image of Christ. Galatians 5:1

says It is for _____ that Christ set us free. Jesus also said in John 8:34

that "everyone who sins is a _____ to sin." Sometimes, it is simply a bad choice. We know better…we simply give in to the impulse of the moment. It isn't habitual…just "one of those things." I'm not giving excuses…we still need to repent for our act of disobedience, and seek forgiveness and cleansing. We also need to take full responsibility for our actions…they were our choice.

This isn't a game… we need to put on the armor He has provided.

There are those things, however, that go deeper than an occasional act. There are addictions, habits, actions, attitudes…areas where we truly want to be free, but there is a force stronger than us at work. Sometimes there has been an attitude or enslavement for generations…we can look back and see our ancestors walking in the same bondage we are experiencing in our lives today. Demonic activity isn't necessarily a result of our own sin…although it may be…we know it says the devil is looking for any actions that allow him entrance. God is a gentleman…he honors our choice. Satan is the opposite of God…he looks for any small opening where he can devise a plan to entrap and imprison us. God calls us to be sober and vigilant. This isn't a game…we need to put on the armor He has provided, standing firm in the truth that God says will set us free. I ask you to consider going back over each lesson and take it seriously…have you left any openings through unforgiveness, unconfessed sin, unbelief, or disobedience? Have you spoken death into areas where you need to repent, and ask the Holy Spirit to guide you in tearing down those fortresses you built, replacing them with life? It is truly for freedom that Christ set us free…He also implores us to stand firm in that freedom, and not allow ourselves to be enslaved again.

WEEK EIGHT - FREEDOM FROM DEMONIC CONTROL

If you find yourself unable to break free from certain areas where you have repented and truly want to change, there is the possibility that demonic forces are at work in your life. The good news is that God gives us clear direction from His word on how to

be set free. Look at Mark 9: 43-47. What does it say you should do if your hand, foot,

or eye causes you to stumble? _____. My

question is this: If you steal, is it your hand that caused you to steal? _____.

Does your foot cause you to go somewhere you shouldn't? _____ I be-

lieve what Jesus is saying here, is we need to get rid of the real problem source in the situation. If it is our own poor choices, then we need to repent and correct our behavior. If, however, it is a force beyond our control, we need to confront the real issue in order to walk in true freedom.

Let me say upfront here, there are issues we can address and find freedom simply by going into our secret place, and dealing with this by ourselves, alone with God. There are other times we need to avail ourselves to the part(s) of the Body that God has gifted with discernment and wisdom necessary to deal with stronger or higher powers. As I share these steps, please be prayerful which way the Holy Spirit would lead you. I encourage you to be willing to humble yourself before others if that is the direction God leads. These steps are in no way all-inclusive, but serve as a guideline to inform us of the possible presence and actions in this area.

One extremely necessary foundational truth is found in Philippians 2:9-11. We need to write it here:

There is no higher name than the name of Jesus. It would do well to review Day 5 of our first week. It sets our foundation firmly on the fact that Jesus is above every ruler, power, authority, and every name that is named. At the name of Jesus, every knee must bow.

With that foundation established, Jesus gives us the first step in Matthew 12: 28-31.

What does verse 29 say we should do? _____. Then what

can we do? _____ In the same way there are angels sent by

God for good, Satan has demons (fallen angels) who seek to do harm. These are the ones Jesus is talking about when He says we can plunder his house.

142

We need to ask God what opened the door for that evil spirit to have entrance into our lives, then repent for opening that door. If it was opened by an ancestral sin, we need to repent on behalf of that ancestor, and any other person that walked in that particular sin.

Once we have repented, we need to receive forgiveness and cleansing. This cancels the right for the evil spirit to continue operating in that area. Deuteronomy 30: 19-20 says, as we choose life we are also choosing it for our descendants. I claim that for my children and grandchildren.

Next, let's look up Matthew 12: 43-45 and write it here. It is lengthy but necessary.

You will need to cooperate with the Holy Spirit, many times fighting against your own understanding/ habits/emotions.

According to verse 43, did the unclean spirit go out? _____. What did he decide to do in verse 44? _____. In 1 John 1:9, what two things does God promise to do when we confess our sins? _____ and _____. Looking back to Matthew 12:44, do you see that once the spirit leaves the area, it needs to be swept and put in order? _____. The problem is that, in addition to being swept and put in order, it is also _____. Once we tell the demon spirit we don't want it anymore (rebuke it/resist it), we need to make sure we invite the Holy Spirit to come into that area and occupy it. Then, when the demon comes back, he will find it swept, put in order, and OCCUPIED.

I want to deal with how we allow the Holy Spirit to occupy that area. Until now, the demon spirit has had full reign. He has trained our mind, will, and emotions in that area. In fact, they are so well trained that they may try to resist the Holy Spirit's truth. Therefore, YOU will need to cooperate with the Holy Spirit, many times fighting against your own understanding/habits/emotions. If you have been trained to react in anger, hurt, or self-pity, you may soon discover you are still responding in that manner. You may be tempted to think the spirit didn't leave. That's why I pointed out the scripture that declares he left. It isn't a problem with the spirit anymore, unless you decide it didn't leave and allow it to come back through wrong thinking.

WEEK EIGHT - FREEDOM FROM DEMONIC CONTROL

Remember, you have an enemy. 2 Corinthians 10:5 is an extremely important and powerful weapon God has given you. Write it here:

The freer you become, the more room there is for the Holy Spirit.

Another scripture is Proverbs 3:5. _____

_____.

You will need to confront every wrong thought and feeling with the word of God. In one sense, this is the harder battle of the two. You MUST win this battle in order to stand firm in the freedom you have received.

There are only two days of study guides for this week. That is not a mistake. Take the next three days to seek the Lord. Ask Him to reveal any areas in your life, or in the lives of your family, where deliverance is needed. Be open, but also be wise. Test everything through the scriptures and wise godly counsel. Use the other weeks' lessons for guidelines to close any open doors to the enemy. Stand on Psalm 129:4. I love the way the Amplified Bible reads:

The freer you become, the more room there is for the Holy Spirit. My desire for you is that you be filled to overflowing with the Holy Spirit, and enjoy His luscious fruit. As I said yesterday...

Freedom – It Tastes So Good!!!

FREEDOM THROUGH INNER HEALING

When a problem remains after prayer, searching our hearts for unforgiveness, unconfessed sin, etc., then many times the root of the problem is deeper than our conscious mind. We need God to reveal the root, and to get rid of it.

God put my _____ on Jesus, that I might become the

_____ of _____ in Him.

I now have a _____ nature.

The law of sin says that the result of sin is _____.

The law of the Spirit says that where the Spirit of the Lord is, there is

_____.

For the law of the _____ in Christ Jesus has set you

free from the law of _____

WEEK NINE - FREEDOM THROUGH INNER HEALING

1. God created _____. Therefore God is _____ of time.

2. God can be in several places at the same _____.

3. God can _____those things that never existed.

4. God can make things that existed as though they _____ existed.

5. God can give _____ to the dead things in your life.

NOTES:

Week Nine - Freedom Through Inner Healing

Have you ever been deeply engrossed in the middle of a movie when, all of a sudden, you see these totally unwelcome words...TO BE CONTINUED...? There is no option but to wait until the next week's episode to find out "who did it?" or "did they survive?"...or whatever the suspense racked storyline leaves hanging. Although you may not have noticed, last week I said I was going to start with a story – "maybe two". This is a continuation of my story...it began with deliverance, but the Holy Spirit told me there was more that would need to be done. I mentioned that freedom did not come suddenly...it actually encompassed a time period of seven years...seven intense years of being shown truth after truth...sometimes choosing quickly – other times seemingly standing and marching in place for what seemed like an eternity. Each step involved TRUTH...truth that had the ability to set me free...if I chose it. Each step also included Emotions and Mindsets that offered familiarity and comfort...with bondage...IF I chose it. I would like to tell you I always chose truth... that is not the case...but I can tell you that God, in the midst of it all, was determined to reveal what that truth looked like, and the promises it contained. As I continued walking with Him, He continued setting me free...one step at a time.

We were fortunate to live in the country and, during this time in life, I found long walks down our country road to be therapeutic to my wounded soul. I remember one of those walks well. Usually, I would begin marching quickly down the road, upset and frustrated with life; but my walk...and especially my talk with God...would minister in such a way that, as I returned from that walk, my pace would be slow and peaceful. Many things were worked out during those walks. This one was different. As I began my walk, I cried out to God, "God, I have no hope". Instantly, I heard in my spirit, "Romans 5:3". Excited to see how God was offering me hope, I immediately turned around, ran into the house, and grabbed my bible. When I began reading that verse and beyond, I became totally upset with God. I thought He would feel sorry for my predicament, and offer me a way out of my situation. Instead, He treated me like the wise Father He is, and basically told me He knew what He was doing, and I needed to let Him have His way.

Each step involved TRUTH...if I chose it. Each step also included Emotions and Mindsets... with bondage... IF I chose it.

He told me He knew what He was doing, and I needed to let Him have His way.

Let's look up Romans 5: 3-5 (NASB). Fill in the blanks:

"...we also _____ in our _____ , knowing that _____

brings about _____ ; and _____ , _____

_____ ; and proven character, _____ ; and HOPE does NOT

_____ ; because the _____ of _____ has been

poured out within our hearts through the Holy Spirit Who was given to us."

Although I would not have chosen tribulation, God was teaching me a great truth

here. In Hebrews 2:10, it says that God would _____ the author of their

salvation (Jesus) through _____. If He could do a necessary work within

Jesus through the suffering He would endure, who was I to be different? Think about it – if Jesus had been able to come and save us without any type of suffering on His behalf, how would that affect the value of the shedding of His blood? The fact that He willingly suffered a horrendous death for you and me adds great value to both His love and our lives. In that sense, God was perfecting the sacrifice that could only be accomplished through great suffering.

There is a work that must be done in each of us if we are to be molded into the image of God's Son.

There is a work that must be done in each of us if we are to be molded into the image of God's Son. Romans 5 says it is in the midst of tribulation where we are given the opportunity to persevere. Without suffering there is no need of perseverance. Even then, it is our choice, but if we will choose perseverance, God says it will produce proven character. There are character flaws within each of us that need to be addressed and conquered; however, without tribulations, those flaws can lay dormant without notice. It is in the midst of hard times that the "real inner issues" reveal themselves. As we allow God to expose and deal with those issues, we are conformed more and more into the image of His Son, and therein lies our hope...because God is pouring out His love within us by cleansing us from everything hindering our sanctification.

It is in the midst of hard times that the "real inner issues" reveal themselves.

We are going to look at Romans 7 in a different way today. I love how God teaches so many different truths out of His word. It is truly living and meets us exactly where we are, to give us life. Let's begin by reading Romans 7:15-25. Most of us are well acquainted and readily identify with verse 15. Paraphrase the last part of that verse:

Woe is me!!! If we stop there, we are simply giving ourselves an excuse to continue in our sin. BUT WAIT...Paul didn't stop there!!! Let's continue. There is hope within this passage. Paul goes on to say, the things God is asking him to do are good. He agrees he should be doing them. What is the issue then? Let's look at verse 17. Write it here:

Now write verse 20:

What is the same theme in both verses? Am I the problem? _____. Paul

is saying I'm NOT the problem! If I'm not the problem, then what does he say is the

real issue? _____. This doesn't let me off the

hook, but it does direct my attention to the real issue. There is a sin issue somewhere
within that needs to be dealt with. In Deuteronomy 30:19, God says He gives us a

_____ between life and death, the blessing and the curse. Would He give us

a choice if it were not within our grasp to choose? Yet here, Paul is saying he is doing
what he doesn't want to do. That tells us the enemy is at work in some way. What

does John 10:10 say the devil wants to do? _____ _____ and

_____. Look at Psalms 140:4-5 (NIV) and fill in the blanks: "Protect me from

the _____, who devise ways to _____ my _____. The

_____ have _____ a _____ for me; they have spread

out the _____ of their _____ and have _____ _____ for

me along my path. Psalm 64: 4-5 says "they shoot from ambush at the innocent; they

shoot suddenly without fear. They encourage each other in evil plans; they talk about
hiding their snares…" Remember 1 Peter 5:8? Paraphrase it here:

We have an enemy who is out to destroy us. He lays snares in secret, and hopes we will
fall into them.

In John 8:34, Jesus shares a necessary concept.

Tomorrow we are going to look at some steps to freedom offered through scripture. For today, take some time to contemplate your life. Ask God to reveal any areas where freedom has evaded you… freedom He longs to give. Ask Him to show you what the real issues are…has the enemy laid a trap?

Remember Galatians 5:1

I see freedom in your future…and it looks amazingly good…

WEEK NINE - FREEDOM THROUGH INNER HEALING

As I journeyed on my path to freedom, inner healing played a major part in my life. Because of that fact, I want to be very intentional in guiding us through this topic. I am, therefore, going to take my video worksheet and cover each area in a thorough, revelatory manner. As we walk through the next few days, it is my prayer that the eyes of your heart will be enlightened, and you will see what is the hope of your calling…true freedom from the inside out.

When a problem remains after prayer, searching our hearts for unforgiveness, unconfessed sin, etc., then many times the root of the problem is deeper than our conscious mind. We need God's Spirit to reveal the root, and to get rid of it.

According to God's word, I should be able to live a sin free life, never giving in to sin or to my flesh. Let's look at 2 Peter 1:3-4 (NASB) and fill in the blanks: "seeing that

His (God's) divine _____ has granted to us _____ pertaining to

_____ and _____, through the true _____ of Him

who called us by His own glory and excellence. For by _____ He has granted to us

His precious and magnificent _____, in order that by them you might

become _____ of the _____ _____, having escaped

the corruption that is in the world by lust." What has he allowed us to become partak-

ers of? _____ _____. Since we have a divine nature, it is no longer

our NATURE to sin, but instead, to live godly lives. Let's turn to Romans 6. The first two

verses tell us it would be foolish to think we should go on sinning since we have died

to sin. Look at verse 6. It says we are no longer _____ to sin. The first sev-

eral verses explain that when we are baptized into Christ, the reality is that we were also baptized into His death and resurrection. Our old sin nature was crucified and no longer lives. Instead, our sinless nature that Peter refers to becomes a reality, not just a nice ethereal thought. Another scripture that bears close examination is 2 Corinthians 5:21. Write it here.

According to God's word, I should be able to live a sin free life, never giving in to sin or to my flesh.

Since we have a divine nature, it is no longer our NATURE to sin.

Coupled with that is 1 Corinthians 1:30.

In order to experience true freedom, we need to uncover the root issue.

Who does it say was responsible for that decision? _____. If it is God's decision that Jesus would take our sins so that we can become possessors of His righteousness, I can rest that it is an unalterable fact. 2 Corinthians 5:17 says it best. Record it here.

We need real answers to real problems.

FACT: OUR OLD SIN LOVING NATURE HAS BEEN CRUCIFIED! WE ARE NOW A NEW CREATURE WITH A SINLESS NATURE.

SO…what about the areas where Romans 7:15 is visibly at work in our lives? Paraphrase that verse here so we have a starting point.

Remember, Jesus said in John 8:34, "everyone who commits sin is a slave of sin". Praise God that He also said He came to set the captives free! (Luke 4:18)

We have learned, in order to experience true freedom, we need to uncover the root issue. In Jeremiah 8:11 God accuses the scribes and leaders of 'healing the brokenness of the daughter of My people superficially by saying 'all is well'; but there is no peace." We don't want to look for superficial answers to our problems. We need real answers to real problems. Let's dig a little deeper…

Week Nine - Freedom Through Inner Healing

Let's go back to Romans 7:22-8:2. Romans 7:22 says my "inner man" delights in God's laws. We know they are good and lead to life. Romans 7:23 (NASB) says "I see a different _____ in the members of my body, waging _____ against the _____ of my mind, and making me a _____ of the _____ of _____ which is in my members." Look at verse 25. There are two laws there. What are they? _____ and _____ Do you see that both verse 23 and 25 speak of the law of sin? _____. Look at Romans 6:23. What does it say are the results of sin? _____.

When we recognize that the law of sin is active in an area of our life (there's something wrong inside of me), we need to also recognize there is a greater law that can set us free. Turn to Romans 8:1-2. At this point in our lives, we desperately need to hear the hope in verse 1. Write it here:

The Lord is not showing us these truths to condemn us; His purpose is to set us free. Many times, when we are in the middle of the battle, we can imagine God is looking down in disappointment and impatience. That is not the case. It is no coincidence He has placed this scripture right in the middle of an intense battle. He wants us to know, not only does He understand; He is the author of hope and freedom. Let's continue… hopefully the next scripture and illustration will plant His truth firmly within our beings.

Fill in the blanks for verse 2. "For the _____ of the _____ of _____ in CHRIST JESUS has _____ you _____ from the _____ of _____ and of _____." Many times we find similarities between natural and spiritual laws. Let's look at one such connection here.

If you drop an apple off the empire state building in New York, the law of gravity will take over, and it will fall to the ground. If you travel to China and drop an apple from the top floor of one of their sky scrapers, the same law of gravity will be in effect in China that was in New York. We understand that no matter where you go, if you drop an apple…or a penny…or any object from any distance, whether it be 100 feet or 2 inches…the law of gravity will cause it to fall to the ground. There is a law of gravity that is constant in the earth. However; in Wichita, Kansas, every day we see airplanes flying in the sky…seemingly defying the law of gravity. It is because they have entered into a higher law…the law of aerodynamics.

WEEK NINE - FREEDOM THROUGH INNER HEALING

Because of the law of aerodynamics, airplanes can fly in the sky every day; however, if they turn off their engines, they will immediately come back under the law of gravity. That tells us that the law of gravity was there all along; there was simply a higher law superseding it…not abolishing it.

There is a law of sin and death: the soul that sins will die. However, there is a higher law of the Spirit of life in Christ Jesus. It does not eliminate the law of sin and death – it supersedes it. It says it sets us free from that law. It does not come through any other way than through Christ Jesus. Look up John 14:6 and write it here.

> **The** law of the Spirit of life in Christ Jesus does not eliminate the law of sin and death – it supersedes it.

Jesus is the ONLY way. When we accept what God has done through Jesus, we enter into that higher law. We have been set free. That is the truth. The scriptures are clear. Jesus has set us free to live above sin and death. Allow that truth to sink deep into your soul.

> **Arm** yourself with the truth that God has provided everything you need for life and godliness.

The truth you know will set you free. Tomorrow we will look at some ways the enemy tries to block that freedom. Truth is your best weapon. Arm yourself with the truth that God has provided everything you need for life and godliness…what an amazingly loving God…

WEEK NINE - FREEDOM THROUGH INNER HEALING

Trauma…something God wants to use in our lives to bring about perseverance, proven character and hope (Romans 5:3-5); a tool used to refine our faith (1 Peter 1:6-7).

Trauma…something the enemy wants to use to bring about fear (King Saul waiting on Samuel), discouragement (Elijah at the river after Jezebel threatened his life), discontentment (David with Bathsheba). A tool used to cause us to doubt God's faithfulness and goodness (Adam and Eve).

Choice…Our decision in every situation that determines whether life or death will flourish and grow in our lives.

Do you get it??? Everything in our life gives us opportunity to grow more and more into the image of Christ (divine nature)…or into the image of the evil one…AND WE CHOOSE…OUCH!!!

God **HAS NOT** given us the sprit of fear (2 Timothy 1:7); discouragement (Romans 15:4); or discontentment (Philippians 4:11). Neither is it His will for us to doubt His faithfulness and goodness. (James 1:17)

God **HAS** given us the freedom and opportunity to choose.

Sometime, when you are in a conversation with a group of friends, try this experiment. When someone is talking, for no apparent reason, clap your hands really loudly, just one time. Where does the attention go? Does it continue with the person's conversation or does it abruptly turn to the loud noise? Most often, everyone's attention will be diverted to the noise. That loud, abrupt noise causes a break in concentration, and brings the focus to the sound. Trauma is like that. It interrupts life and puts everything on hold, sometimes superseding the truth you know. It is a powerful force that the enemy hopes will successfully demand all your attention.

The enemy wants to use this to funnel our attention away from God's goodness and provision, and place it onto fear… fear for safety, finances, loved ones, relationships, health. Trauma tends to take over our lives, causing everything else to fade to the background of our minds. Yet, God's Word invites us to a higher plane…it shows us a safety net against trauma. In Philippians 4:6 we find a 2-step exercise towards peace. Write it here:

The enemy wants to use this to funnel our attention away from God's goodness and provision, and place it onto fear.

God's Word invites us to a higher plane.

Week Nine - Freedom Through Inner Healing

What is the first step…DON'T BE _____. Second step tells us what to

do: _____. 1 Corinthians 10:13 gives us

a promise. It tells us that any time we are tempted, God _____

_____. When we experience trauma, we are tempted to give in to fear. What is

God's way of escape that we just saw in Philippians 4:6? _____

_____. As we pray, the Holy Spirit is able to remind us that God desires to use the

hard times in our lives to conform us into the image of His Son. The next verse tells us what will happen if we pray. Write verse 7 here.

What we choose will determine whether we walk in the blessing or the curse

Once there is an opening where the enemy is allowed, he has a right to remain, unless that reason is addressed and resolved.

Peace is the opposite of fear. Trauma presents the same results as a loud hand clap. When that happens, we reach a "choice point". What we choose will determine whether we walk in the blessing or the curse…and each choice we make will affect our future generations.

This is our answer for present and future "life calamities" we might face. The question that now arises is, "what about traumatic experiences in our childhood that have already occurred?" We realize that, since our choices affect our offspring, the choices our ancestors made have had a tremendous, although perhaps hidden, impact on our lives as well. One of the ways the enemy lays a trap for us is through physical, emotional, or mental abuse. It can be purposefully or innocently done. It can be aimed directly at us, or the result of abuse in past generations. Those can cause openings for the enemy to continue producing bondage for generations to come. Proverbs 26: 2 tells us an underserved curse does not come to rest. Once there is an opening where the enemy is allowed, he has a right to remain unless that reason is addressed and resolved. As we learned in Day One of this week, Satan schemes to lay snares in secret. Let me share two true stories with you to illustrate this fact.

A young middle school girl struggled with her image. She was a victim of insecurity and hated everything about herself. She came to me for prayer, and as we prayed, God revealed that she had been victimized by her classmates. Children can be cruel, sometimes on purpose. Some of her classmates had made a habit of calling her names; one of them was that she looked like a witch. She had allowed those words to cut deep within her being and actually create a false statement of her value. As we took those words captive, and called them what they were – lies of the enemy – and accepted what God said about her in Psalms 139: 13-15, she received healing in her soul. Several weeks later, I saw her and excitedly she showed me her new shoes. I failed to see the significance in the shoes until she shared that, up to this time, she had been unable to wear pointed toed shoes because they confirmed to her that she was, indeed, the witch her classmates had proclaimed her to be. Now, however, she had been set free to walk in the truth and freedom…proven by the fact that she didn't even realize the shoes were pointed, until long after she had purchased and begun wearing them. This is a seemingly insignificant story…unless you are the one who had received - and accepted - the label the enemy had given you. Blessed freedom…proven by a pair of shoes!

One more story…this is a painful one for me to share, because it is about me. As I have shared, I struggled with being an unfit mom. I accepted Jesus as my Lord when our third child was only two months old and, much to my dismay, continued struggling with anger and rejection issues. When I found out a few months later that I was pregnant with our fourth child, I was beside myself. I didn't know how I would ever handle a fourth child when I was struggling so much with the three I now had. Of course, when our precious daughter was born, all of that vanished. She was such a beautiful blessing, and I was incredibly grateful. God was so gracious to give me an amazing gift He knew I would prize and cherish. Not long after that, however, I began seeing signs of rebellion and a wrong spirit operating in her life. At 18 months old, she was definitely contrary to anything I asked of her…not your ordinary childhood development where a child tries the boundaries, and learns obedience is better than discipline. It didn't matter what I said or did, she was noticeably defiant. One afternoon, as she was napping on the floor, I knelt down and cried out to God…"God, what is wrong with my little one? Why is she acting this way towards me? Please help me…help her." The Holy Spirit spoke directly to my heart, "You rejected her when she was in your womb, and when you did that, you opened her up to a spirit of rejection. When that spirit of rejection came in, it also opened the door for another spirit, a spirit of retaliation: "Oh, you don't want me…well, I'll show you!" I was heartbroken to realize what my rejection did to my precious little one. I begged for, and received, forgiveness; then laid my hands on my sleeping little girl and prayed deliverance over her.

Several months passed, and I forgot the incident…sometimes, when we experience relief, we forget how fierce the battle really was. One day, I was sitting with a friend while our children were playing together, when she commented, "Your little girl is the sweetest little girl I have ever seen. There is such a sweetness about her…such a sweet spirit." I realized then that she had been set totally free…even free to this day, where she is one of the sweetest young women you will ever meet. Freedom…given in spite of a mother who fell into a trap set to destroy both her and her daughter. What a precious God we serve!

When we or our loved ones have been entrapped in a sinful lifestyle, and truly want freedom, God offers a way out.

When we or our loved ones have been entrapped in a sinful lifestyle, and truly want freedom, God offers a way out. We need to ask the Holy Spirit to show us if there is a sin principle that has been implanted into our lives by the enemy. 2 Corinthians 3:17 gives us a promise. Write that verse here.

WEEK NINE - FREEDOM THROUGH INNER HEALING

If we are truly a child of God, the Holy Spirit wants to bring freedom into every area of our lives. Because God has said He honors our choices, we need to cooperate with Him as He shows us areas where we lack victory over sin… whether big or small. We need to use the same weapon Jesus used against the enemy…the Word of God.

THE WAY OF ESCAPE

**First comes the need to repent for any part we, or any ancestor, had in allowing the enemy entrance, and ask for forgiveness and cleansing. James 4:8-10 (NASB) is our guide. _____ _____ to God;... _____ your hands, _____ your hearts…Be _____ and _____ . In your own words, what does that look like? _____

_____ (that leads to true repentance).

**Once we mourned over our sin, I John 1:9 is our next step:

What two things does God say He will do if we confess our sins? _____

_____ The question then is, do I believe He has forgiven and cleansed me from the sin I've confessed?

Have I accepted that? _____

** A question we need to ask at this point is this – Am I willing to be completely free in this area? That might sound like a foolish question, but it is an honest question. If we are honest, there are times we would rather glory in our affliction than to walk in freedom. We love the accolades or the sympathy afforded by the world, rather than to receive the freedom Christ offers. Until we truly desire freedom, we cannot go any further.

**The next step is to accept the way of escape. The Law of the Spirit of Life in Christ Jesus is greater than the law of sin and death. (I don't have to stay in my sin. There is a way out of this through Jesus Christ.)

**Admit that we don't necessarily know what the root of the problem is. (Proverbs16:2:

The ways of a man are _____ in his own sight; Proverbs 16:25:

There is a way that seems _____ to a man, but its end is the way of

_____.

**Psalm. 139:23,24 This is where we need the Spirit that searches all things, (I Corinthians 2:10). We need to pray for God's Holy Spirit to search our very depths, and see if there is any hurtful way in us - either hurtful to us, or to others, or to God. Sometimes we don't recognize it as sin. When something sinks into our subconscious, the only way it comes out is by dealing with it in our conscious mind, and throwing it out.

**Deuteronomy 30:19 Choose Life. God says the powers of heaven and earth are watching our choice. We empower the one we choose.

God created us and cares about our TOTAL being - spirit, body, and soul (mind, will and emotions). He wants us to be completely whole in all these areas, and only He knows how one area may be related to another.

INNER HEALING PRAYER

First pray, thanking God for Who He is: All-loving (He loves you so much that He wants to set you free), all-wise (He knows exactly what needs to be done in order for you to be set free), and all-powerful (He is powerful enough to set you free). Ask Him for His guidance through His Holy Spirit and for His protection from any spirits of darkness that would seek to lead you astray. OPENLY accept God's will, and resist anything from Satan, in the name of Jesus.

Ask God to go back with you to the very time you were conceived in your mother's womb, and walk with you, moment by moment, revealing if necessary, any hurts or sins that have imbedded themselves in your mind or emotions, and have held you in bondage in one form or another. Perhaps someone said something, or did something to you that caused you to be afraid to reach out to others for fear of being hurt again. Perhaps it's a different type of fear, caused by an incident in your early childhood, a fear that manifests itself in your being afraid of circumstances – a dark night, a certain animal, insects, cars, airplanes, long trips, heights, water, close places, loud noises; maybe fears of insecurity, financially or emotionally; fear of losing your spouse or their love, your friends, etc. Sometimes, because of things that happen in our childhood, we find it difficult or impossible to function normally in an area of our lives, and don't know why. Maybe we aren't the kind of husband or wife we want to be, or the father or mother, or the friend. Perhaps we can't keep a confidence entrusted to us, or we have a critical spirit we can't seem to control. These are legitimate problems, and there are many more – inability to love our parents or brothers or sisters. Only God knows your individual problem. YOU don't even know it in its depths and root. But as God reveals them to you, take time to do three things.

1. Stop and honestly consider if you had any part in that incident - if you sinned in any way, and ask God to reveal it to you if you did. Then ask His forgiveness for that part.

2. Look at that incident openly, and see if anyone else had sinned against you in that incident. If there is any need to forgive anyone, don't go any further until you have forgiven them.

3. Ask God to destroy the root of that problem, forgive anyone involved, and cleanse it from your life.

Continue through your life with God revealing things to you. Be open and accept what He shows you. He wants to free you; and not hurt you. Claim your freedom from sin indwelling you, and accept the forgiveness and cleansing power of God. Claim Romans 8:2.

Ask God to fill all of the cleansed, empty places in your life with the Holy Spirit. This is very necessary to keep Satan from re-entering that area. Matthew 12: 43.

God takes us through various depths of inner healing. Once is probably not enough. It simply removes the top layer of hurts. Each time He can go a little deeper. Be open to His leading about doing this again in the future.

--- When you come up against another problem, then what? ---

1. Confess it as sin and ask forgiveness for what you are doing, or for what you have done to cause the situation.

2. Ask God to take you back to the root of your problem, deal with it, destroy it, forgive and cleanse you, and then fill that area with His Holy Spirit.

FREEDOM
A Beautiful Choice!

FREEDOM FROM UNGODLY SOUL TIES

2 Timothy 2: 20-21 We are the ones who _____ what type of

_____ we will be.

God created us for _____

_____ with HIM and _____ with each other.

Whenever we enter into a relationship with another person, we give that person a part of ourselves – the extent of that depends upon the depth of the relationship.

Genesis 2:23-24 The Strongest Human Form of Soul Tie is meant to be between a

_____ and _____.

I Corinthians 6:15-20 Uniting through fornication also makes the _____

become _____ flesh.

Hebrews 13:4 Let the marriage bed be _____.

Any type of activity accompanied by _____ and

_____ is perverted. Perversion becomes a habitual

force, always demanding more perversion.

Another devastating consequence of fornication is the _____ of

evil spirits.

163

Week Ten - Freedom From Ungodly Soul Ties

Satan knows if he can get a person into a _____ situation, he can freely transfer all manners of defiling spirits to them.

God is a God of _____ and

_____.

I John 3:8 Jesus came to _____ the works of the devil.

Romans 4:17 God is able to _____ those things that never existed.

I Corinthians 1:28 God is able to _____ the things that currently exist.

NOTES:

WEEK TEN - FREEDOM FROM UNGODLY SOUL TIES

Ties...all of us experience ties in our lives...emotional ties to friends/enemies...financial ties to loaning institutions or savings accounts...physical ties...business ties...relational ties to ancestors, alive as well as gone on before us. Each person or place has impacted our lives in one way or another. In a sense, they make us or determine who we are and how far we can go in life. Bank accounts...or lack thereof...determine the type of home we purchase and the kind of vehicle we drive. Family ties can relegate us to the right or wrong side of the tracks. Ties...good and bad, we all have them. Since they have such an impact on our lives, it would do well to examine them to determine which are blessings or detriments...if there are ties we should keep, and if there are some we should break.

In this lesson we are going to study ties that affect the "real me"...the ones that go straight for our heart. There is a saying, "just follow your heart." If we are going to do that, we need to make sure we have an undivided heart towards God. As Paul says in 1 Corinthians 11:1, KJV: "Be ye followers of me, even as I also am of Christ." That's what our heart needs to be able to say; however, in order for that to happen, it needs to be free of the chains and cords that would try to bind it or head it in the wrong direction.

Ties...good and bad, we all have them.

Let's look at some different types of ties/cords, and what their purpose is. We can then determine what action should be taken...welcoming them into our soul or throwing them into the deep abyss.

Start by checking out Psalm 18:4-5. Record it here:

Were those good or bad chords? _____ What did David do when he found

himself in this situation? _____

Paraphrase God's response to his cry. (Verses 16-19)

WEEK TEN - FREEDOM FROM UNGODLY SOUL TIES

God's plan is to free us from the cords the enemy wants to use to drag us to the depths of hell. One of the ways He does this is found in verses 33-36. Who does God plan to use to win the battle? (Verses 37-42) _____ Sometimes we want someone else to come and fight our battles for us. God's plan is to equip us and then instruct us how and when to fight the battle. It would be good to read all of Psalm 18. It is one of my favorites.

Speaking of instructing and training, Proverbs 5:21-23 are pretty straightforward verses. Write out verse 22:

God's plan is to equip us and then instruct us how and when to fight the battle.

What kind of cords was this man dealing with? _____ Would those be cords we want to keep or throw into the pit? _____

_____ This shows us that the enemy is ruthless and is determined to capture and destroy us. Praise God that He is waiting to hear our cry, and so willing to come to our rescue. BEWARE HOWEVER, too late is too late. Remember Proverbs 1:23-33. Take time to read it…it's pretty straight-forward in its teaching.
Job gives us some insights into the strategy God used in creating the heavens.

Job 38:31-33 speaks of how God formed the constellations and even has seasons for them to reveal themselves to us on the earth. He has bound together each star with the other to form what we see today. Write verse 33.

It speaks of God's careful, intentional laws and boundaries in the heavens. If He is that intentional for inanimate objects, think how intentional His love and power is towards us who believe!!! His cords of love are meant to bring life and order into our world. The enemy wants only destruction.

Let's look at Jesus. He actually used cords as a weapon against ungodliness. John 2:14-16 tells the story. What did He use cords to do? _____

_____. His intent was to cleanse the temple. That's the only reason cords should be allowed in our lives…to make our temple cleaner and closer to portraying the image of Christ.

One last area for today. Ecclesiastes 4: 9-12 speaks of the power of unity. God did not create us to walk alone. He made that plain in the garden when He created a "helper" for Adam. (Genesis 2:18). This was someone to help him when he fell down and yet one whom he could lift up if she fell down. This isn't talking about marriage at this point… it is simply saying we all need those who will walk alongside of us in this journey called life. Ecclesiastes 4 agrees. Paraphrase the benefits of having two walking together.

We all need those who will walk alongside of us in this journey called life.

What is the danger of walking alone? _____

_____In addition to this, I want to draw out a point

of interest here. Verse 12 speaks of a battle…someone trying to overpower a person. What does it say if there are two of you? _____

Two indeed are better than one, BUT…what does it say about a cord of three strands?

_____ The difference between two and three

If you don't know there is an enemy, you won't know you need to fight him.

standing together could be considered exponential. Look at Deuteronomy 32:30. How

many can one put to flight? _____ What about two? _____. Just

imagine adding one more to that group…however, be careful…different strand combinations have different strengths…1 Corinthians 15:33 gives us a warning. Write it here:

BEWARE…The enemy would love to bring that "third person" that would weaken the cord instead of strengthening it.

Tomorrow we will look at some of the cords the enemy wants to use in our personal lives. As we have said before, if you don't know there is an enemy, you won't know you need to fight him.

Emotions...what do we do with them?...what would we do without them??? They can brighten our day or frighten our day. We would agree that without them life is dreary and dull but too many of them will push us into a maize of drama. We know they are good because God created them in us. However, we need to take a closer look to see how the enemy can use them to bind us into relationships that are destructive, both to us and the other person. What do we need to know about emotions in reference to soul ties?

The Psalms are full of emotion. Time and time again David cried out to the Lord in his distress; yet, many other times found him singing praises to his Lord and King. Let's begin with Psalms 107. What emotion is seen in the first two verses?

_____.

What emotions would you find in verses 5-6? _____.

What does He promise to do in verse 9 for the soul that is thirsty and hungry?

_____. Now turn to Psalm 23...that very familiar Psalm we

all love. Who is the one in verse 3 that restores our soul? _____ List three

ways in verses 2-3 that He restores our soul. _____

_____   _____.

God desires to be the one we turn to when our souls are hungry, thirsty or need rest.

God desires to be the one we turn to when our souls are hungry, thirsty or need rest.

It is true that many times people are God's hands and feet; however, remember 1 Corinthians 15:33 from yesterday. We need to be very careful who we turn to for comfort. Whenever we enter into a relationship with another person we end up giving that person a part of ourselves – the extent of that depends upon the depth of the relationship.

I love to have coffee with friends...I especially like one on one times, where it is safe to be transparent and share more intimately. Those times are so needed in our lives.

Proverbs 27:17 says _____.

I love it when we begin talking about Jesus and the things the Holy Spirit has been teaching us...it is exhilarating, and I leave refreshed and encouraged in my walk. Not all times are like that, of course. There are times we share our struggles, our concerns, our needs. Even then, though, there is a sense of drawing closer to the Lord as we promise to pray for each other or, sometimes we stop right then and there and pray.

The truth is...when I leave those meetings, I find myself leaving a little piece of my heart/soul with that friend...and I have a little piece of hers. That's just how life was meant to be. We are all meant to be a part of one another...all individual parts of the same Body. Write Romans 12:5

God wants to use the godly ties to advance HIS Kingdom; satan wants to use the ungodly ones to advance HIS kingdom.

Paul is talking to Christians here. 2 Corinthians 6:14-15 speaks of our fellowship with non-believers. Paraphrase it here:

NASB says "Don't be BOUND together. Whoever you "partner with" is going to leave something in your life, and you are going to give them a part of you. That's where soul ties are formed. God wants to use the godly ties to advance HIS Kingdom; satan wants to use the ungodly ones to advance HIS kingdom.

Perhaps now would be a good time to think about those relationships in your life... which ones are healthy, godly ties? Might need to check if there are any unhealthy, ungodly ones that need to be removed. The choice we make determines whose kingdom we are advancing.

Although I love those "coffee times" with friends, I absolutely cherish late night visits when loved ones come to stay a few days. Our daytimes are filled with little ones and all sorts of activities. Adult conversation is monitored throughout the day...lots of little eyes and ears require sharing to be kept on a lighter, more surface level. BUT when evening comes and little ones are gently tucked in bed, it becomes "Tea Time". Tea time is different than coffee time. Coffee time usually involves close friends who share their story and listen to mine. I love coffee time and adore my friends. Tea time, however, is a time of family coming together and sharing OUR story together. It is a time of walking hand in hand...sharing deeply with no time limits. We simply share until we are finished. I absorb everything I can during those Tea Times. Days afterwards I am still remembering them, still allowing things to settle deep within. Every tea time changes who I am...clear down to my soul. Family ties are definitely a part of the soul tie spectrum. I'm thankful for my beautiful family. I love our ties... however, I know others are not as fortunate. They must fight for freedom from ties that would strangle, condemn, and imprison.

Through our study we have learned to forgive...to speak life instead of death...to appropriate healing and deliverance to those areas in our lives that have been violated. Now we must address the area of soul ties.

A soul tie is the knitting together of two souls that can either bring tremendous blessings or tremendous destruction.

A soul tie is the knitting together of two souls that can either bring tremendous blessings in a godly relationship or tremendous destruction when made with the wrong person. The stronger the soul tie, the more we become like those to whom we relate.

In a good soul tie, the mental and emotional strength of one sustains the other in times of adversity and allows them to rejoice with the other in times of triumph. When the love between friends is pure and not polluted by any selfish desire, the bond between them works for good in their lives. Look up John 15:13 and write it here:

Proper godly soul ties are an enormous benefit to both parties involved.

For an example of a good soul tie, read 1 Samuel 18: 1-4 (NASB). David had just finished killing Goliath. There was something about David that King Saul's son, Jonathan

deeply loved. Verse 1 says the _____ of Jonathan was _____ to the

_____ of David. Recognizing the divine call upon David, Jonathan gladly

relinquished his right to inherit the throne of Israel to his friend. David benefited greatly from their close soul tie. After Saul and Jonathan's deaths, David became king. 2 Samuel 9: 1-13 tells the story of David honoring his covenant with Jonathan by bringing Jonathan's son into his palace, setting him a place at David's table, and restoring all the land that belonged to him. Proper godly soul ties are an enormous benefit to both parties involved.

Another example of a good soul tie is found in Ruth 1: 15-18. (The book of Ruth is only 4 chapters in length…it would make a good read.) Naomi had come from Bethlehem with her husband and two sons, and settled in the land of Moab. Both of her sons married Moabite women, then all three men died. After some time Naomi determined to return to Bethlehem. She pleaded with her daughter-in-laws to return to their fathers' homes. Orpah returned, but Ruth gave up her own family and abandoned her homeland, in order to follow and serve her mother-in-law, Naomi. Because of their deep bond, both women benefited. Ruth was received in Bethlehem because of Naomi; Naomi was provided food and sustenance as Ruth gleaned in the fields; Naomi's redeemer became Ruth's redeemer; Ruth is now in the lineage of Jesus; and Naomi became the rightful legal grandmother of Obed, the grandfather of David.

In a deep and true friendship like the one between David and Jonathan, or Ruth and Naomi, each party remains giving, faithful, and loyal, even to his own hurt. Self-sacrificing soul ties like these form the basis of enduring friendships.

These examples were between two men and between two women. Pure soul ties can exist between same sex individuals with God's blessing. Many women have other women as best friends; men have other men as comrades. We must be aware, however, and always cognizant of the possibility of those ties crossing over the line into ungodly soul ties. God declares in I Peter 1:16:

Romans 1: 18-32 is a severe warning that must be heeded.

It would be good to summarize II Timothy 2: 20-21:

Who determines what kind of vessel we will become? _____ How do we put

that into daily practice? _____

_____

_____

One last scripture for this session is found in Acts 4:32 (NASB). Summarize the verse:

Here, the bond of unity was so strong and their hearts were so pure that they freely shared all their possessions with one another.

Whenever we enter into a relationship with another person we end up giving that person a part of ourselves – the extent of that depends upon the depth of the relationship. We can become soul tied to those related to us, associates at work, contacts in the social realm, or those to whom we submit. Because our soul ties are so influential in shaping our lives, we need to carefully examine our relationships and friendships.

When we become bonded to someone whose motives are impure or selfish, the soul tie can become an avenue for manipulation and abuse. We can actually become controlled . Our mind, will and emotions become instruments where the soul ties act as channels into our lives, producing emotional and mental bondage. Even in seemingly good relationships, ungodly soul ties can develop if those relationships are not in divine order. God demands first place in our hearts, followed by our spouse, then children, family and associates. When our strongest soul tie is to God, there is a divine covering and protection that can help us to withstand forming ungodly soul ties. In Psalm 62:5 the psalmist speaks to his soul, saying, "my soul, wait in silence for God only, for my hope is from Him." He is commanding his soul to be tied only to God. In a wrong soul tie, we look to the other person to meet our needs. Even when we are the one "meeting the need", our soul is dependent upon that other person needing us. Our soul becomes tied in an emotional web to that other person. If the relationship is pure, the soul tie can be very beneficial, but if the relationship is not healthy then the tie becomes bondage.

CHOICES – LIFE OR DEATH – BLESSING OR CURSE – ALL OURS TO MAKE...

When we become bonded to someone whose motives are impure or selfish, the soul tie can become an avenue for manipulation and abuse.

173

Strongest Human Form of Soul Tie

"Soul tie" in the bible can be described by the word knit, or by the word cleave. Cleave means "to bring close together, follow close after, be attached to someone, or adhere to one another as with glue". Let's look up Deuteronomy 10:20 (NASB)

Without first cleaving to God... nothing else can fall into its proper place.

Putting things in the correct order is a necessary first step. Without first cleaving to God...recognizing Him as our very life...nothing else can fall into its proper place. As we have learned, God desires our undivided heart. James 1:7-8 says a divided heart keeps us from hearing and receiving from the Lord.

Today we are going to dig deep...some of the topics may be a little uncomfortable but they are oh, so necessary. Stay with me...you'll be glad you did.

Read Genesis 2:23-24 and Matthew 19:4-6 and summarize them:

When two people marry, they actually become one. Marriage soul ties were never meant to be broken. The tie is so powerful that it allows each partner to absorb both the best and worst from each other. Divorce rips apart two intertwined souls. The intermingled cords cannot be separated without inflicting deep wounds upon one another. It is impossible to simply go separate ways with all emotions in tact. However, there are times when divorce is necessary. When that happens, we need to know how to deal with those broken places. As we continue reading we will address that issue.

Another issue that needs to be addressed begins in Roman 11:16

The root must be holy for the rest to be holy. If the marriage relationship has started out on an impure foundation, God requires repentance so He can cleanse and begin on His pure foundation. Too many times, couples think that even though they were promiscuous with each other before marriage, now that the wedding has occurred, they are somehow cleansed from everything in their past. The Lord will not build on an unholy foundation. That can be a root cause of many future marital problems and must be addressed as a root issue. Write Hebrews 13:4

The root must be holy for the rest to be holy.

It is clear that God says He will judge those who have engaged in any sexual defilement. Any type of activity accompanied by lustful thoughts and unclean fantasy, whether in or outside of marriage, is perverted and will not satisfy. Instead, it becomes a habitual force in the person's life, always demanding more perversion. Repentance is the only answer for this. If this is an issue in your life, you may want to turn to the repentance guideline given at the end of the lesson on Unconfessed Sin.

The next issue is extremely important. It is one of the most common causes of deep soul ties. Turn to 1 Corinthians 6: 15-20. This scripture is speaking to Christians here but the truth is for all to see and beware. God said that when a man & woman are married they become one flesh. **BUT LOOK AT 1 CORINTHIANS 6:16.** Write it here:

Inside or outside of marriage, when a person has intimate physical relations with another person, they become one flesh.

Inside or outside of marriage, when a person has intimate physical relations with another person, they become one flesh. They cannot simply be separated and go their own way. Each will give the other a part of themselves, and leave with a part of the other person. Even if it is a "one-night stand", this is a scriptural law that cannot be broken.

There is tremendous strength in the physical union between a man and a woman. Proverbs 5: 20-23 serves as a warning. Summarize it here.

Let's look at a situation where a woman has relations with one or more men before marriage. The men she has relations with have also had relations with other women – or men. The man she is going to marry also had relations with one or more women who have had relations with one or more women or men...... now, they marry one another.

They have given so many pieces of themselves to others, and have taken so many parts of the other persons, that they are unable to enter into a marriage partnership and give themselves completely. They no longer possess all of themselves anymore - they are fragmented. On their wedding night, they are not just bringing themselves to the marriage bed, but also all the others they have known......**and the marriage bed is defiled from the beginning.**

If the marriage or affair ends, they never walk away in tact. Instead, they are carrying part of the other person with them. It is the same as securely gluing two pieces of wood together. If you try to pull them apart, they will not break where they were glued, but will fragment, leaving parts of each piece with the other.

God designed women to desire their first partner (supposing this would be their husband) and that she would be mysteriously tied to him. This can lead the woman to be drawn back to the first man she had relations with, even if it wasn't her husband, causing devastating consequences in her marriage.

Transference of Evil Spirits
Another devastating consequence of fornication is the transference of evil spirits. Because the two are now one, the evil spirits can move freely between them. Rape can also be an avenue of transference of evil spirits. Many times homosexuality is the result of a homosexual molestation as a child. As the two become "one flesh", the evil spirits have access to the other person's soul (not their spirit). Satan knows if he can get a person into a compromising situation, he can freely transfer all manners of defiling spirits to them, even destroying the very work the Lord has given them to do.

Let's go back to that couple that had several relationships with others before they married. Not only were they soul tied, but they had also allowed evil spirits to be transferred during those times. Perhaps one of the partners (or the partner's previous partners) had a spirit of lust...perhaps anger...addiction...homosexuality. Because of the ability for those spirits to transfer to that person, they now bring those into the marriage bed. When they "become one" with their marriage partner, those spirits are then transferred to them. For an example, let's take homosexuality. We find it happening more and more often today that married couples divorce and then, down the road they both enter into homosexual relationships. One of the ways that could happen is that one of them had a sexual relationship with someone with that spirit before marriage...devastating consequences caused by disobeying God's command to keep the marriage bed undefiled.

Satan knows if he can get a person into a compromising situation, he can freely transfer all manners of defiling spirits to them.

WEEK TEN - FREEDOM FROM UNGODLY SOUL TIES

I read a story of a young woman who dated a guy in high school. Her intentions were to stay pure but she soon gave in to his pressure to become physically intimate. She reasoned that they would be married soon, so it was ok; however, during her senior year she became a Christian and broke off the relationship, thinking everything would be over. She attended college and met a wonderful Christian man, fell in love and they were married. At first it was a wonderful relationship, but she soon began fanaticizing about her former boyfriend. Her desire was to be with him instead of her husband, whom she truly loved. In fact, the desire was so intense she was afraid if she saw him again, she would be powerless to resist him.

A Christian counselor taught her about soul ties, and with repentance and the help of her husband, she was set free. She learned that since God's intention is for the physical union to first be experienced in marriage, He designed the woman to desire her first partner above all else (Genesis 3:16). That understandably creates a problem when the first partner is someone other than her husband. Instead of being able to give herself completely to her spouse, she continues to desire and be enamored with her first encounter.

So how do we break free if we have allowed this bondage to come into our lives?

God can take those who have been shattered and defiled through sexual and worldly involvement and restore them to innocence and purity through the redemptive work of Jesus on the cross. Let's look up some scriptures (NASB) that will give us hope and direction.

Psalm 129:4 "The Lord is _____. He has _____ ___

_____"We need to ask God to

cut the wicked cords that have us bound.

I John 3:8 (last part of verse) "The Son of God appeared for this purpose, that He ____

_____" There are no chains the

enemy has used in your life that Jesus can't destroy.

Rom 4:17 (last part of verse) "God, Who gives _____

and calls into being that which _____

God can make those things that" never were" to be as though they "always were".

I Corinthians 1:28 "God has chosen the base things of the world and the despised, God

has chosen the things that _____ _____ that He might _____

the things that are." God can take things in your life and make them as though they never were there.

WEEK TEN - FREEDOM FROM UNGODLY SOUL TIES

Matt 18:18 "Whatever you _____ (forbid) on earth shall be _____ (forbidden) in heaven and whatever you _____ (permit) on earth is _____ (permitted) in heaven." God has given us the authority to forbid the enemy from working.

Again, true repentance is the key to freedom. I have included a sample prayer. Feel free to personalize your prayer as the Holy Spirit leads and directs you down the path to cleansing and freedom. If you have been involved in more than one illicit relationship, be sure to pray over each one individually, if possible.

Again, true repentance is the key to freedom.

PRAYER:

"Father, in the name of Jesus, I submit my soul, my desires and my emotions to Your Spirit. I confess, as sin, all my promiscuous, premarital sexual relationships, and all sexual relationships outside of marriage. I confess all my ungodly spirit, soul, and body ties as sin. I thank You for forgiving me and cleansing me right now!

"Father, thank You for giving me the keys of Your kingdom, the keys of spiritual authority. What I bind is bound and what I loose is loosed. In Jesus' name, I ask You to loose me from all soulish ties to past sexual partners and ungodly relationships. Please uproot all the tentacles of sexual bondage, of emotional longings and dependencies, and of enslaving thoughts. I bind, renounce, and resist any evil spirits that have reinforced those soul ties or may have been transferred to me through evil associations.

"God, I recognize I sinned (or was sinned against) when _____. I choose to forgive that person who sinned against me. I want to break the bond that I made with _____ and I break that in Jesus' Name.

"I call that part of myself that's been attached to _____ back to me through the blood of Jesus Christ, and I send that part of _____ back to them. "God, thank You for making me whole.

"Please cleanse my soul and help me to forget all illicit unions so that I am free to give my soul totally to You and to my mate. Father, I receive Your forgiveness for all past sex sins. I believe I am totally forgiven. Thank You for remembering my sins no more. Thank You for cleansing me from all unrighteousness. I commit myself totally to You. By Your grace, please keep me holy in my spirit, soul, and body. I praise You. In Jesus' Name, Amen!!!"

Thank you for joining me on this journey. My prayer is that your life will be forever changed through the truths you have experienced through this ten-week study. Please feel free to visit my website www.nancytantonministries.com.

Made in the USA
Columbia, SC
02 April 2021